The Art of Advocacy
A Parent's Guide to a Collaborative IEP Process

Charmaine Thaner M.A.

Text copyright © 2015 by Charmaine Thaner

All Rights Reserved

No part of this book may be reproduced or transmitted in any form or by any means, electronic or mechanical, including photocopying, recording, or by an information storage and retrieval system without express written permission from the author.

Disclaimer:

No portion of this material is intended to offer legal advice. The author is not an attorney. Therefore, the contents of this book, in its entirety, should not be construed as legal advice, but, rather the opinion of the author.

The information contained herein cannot replace or substitute for the services of trained professionals in any field, including, but not limited to legal matters. Under no circumstances, including but not limited to negligence, will Charmaine Thaner, or Collaborative Special Education Advocacy be liable for any special or consequential damages that result from the use of, or the inability to use, the materials, information, or strategies communicated through these materials, or any services following these materials, even if advised of the possibility of such damages.

Author Contact Information

Charmaine Thaner

charmaine@cspeda.com

www.cspeda.com

With Gratitude

To my wonderfully supportive husband, Jim whose reminders to breath and keep it simple, help me to keep on keepin' on!

To my determined son, Dylan whose extraordinary gifts have allowed me to know the beauty of the invisible.

To my wise daughter Nicole who told me when Dylan was a baby that I was wrong when I wasn't sure what Dylan would accomplish. She knew to believe Dylan could do much more than people were expecting.

To my sensitive son Matthew who is that big brother that Dylan still adores today.

May we all have family that love and support us!

Contents

Start Here 1

Chapter 1: **Conflict and Collaborative Advocacy** 7

Chapter 2: **Listen and Ask Questions with Genuine Curiosity** 23

Chapter 3: **How To Listen With Your Eyes** 40

Chapter 4: **Know What to Say When** 47

Chapter 5: **Building Authentic Relationships** 65

Chapter 6: **How To Use Collaborative Problem Solving** 89

Chapter 7: **The End is Really the Beginning** 112

Start Here

When walking down the school hallway to go to an IEP meeting, have you had that queasy feeling in your stomach, a dry throat, and a pounding heart? You take a deep breath, turn the doorknob and walk into a crowded conference room. You feel a little awkward; like you do not belong. After finding a seat, you quickly sit down, laying your notebook on the table. The meeting starts with introductions and then the round robin reporting of test scores. The scene is a blur. The conversation is filled with special education jargon. Long lists of what the student cannot do are shared. You clear your throat because you know it is going to be your turn to talk soon. You begin by sharing what she can do, the importance of having high expectations, and suggestions for meaningful IEP goals.

The special education director reminds the group how it is best to only write goals of what the student will be able to achieve. The director and the rest of the team look surprised as you explain why you believe your goals are realistic and why it is important to have high expectations. A polite debate begins, but you know how important it is to stand strong.

As the conversation continues, you have your doubts that a positive outcome for the student will happen. At the end of the meeting you ask the special education director what is the next step since you disagree with the IEP as written. The director gives you that sideward glance, as if he is saying, "You aren't going to go there are you?"

Does any of this sound familiar? Have you been to IEP meetings when you felt hesitant but knowing you had to speak up? I've been there too. The scenario above describes one of my first IEP meetings I attended as a special education teacher. I was a young teacher, passionate about advocating for my students. I felt a duty to speak up for my students because I knew they could do much more than people gave them credit for.

Fast forward sixteen years, my husband and I are sitting at a long conference table, with queasy stomachs, dry throats and pounding hearts. Yes, this time we were parents at the IEP meeting. Even though both my husband and I were special education teachers, the conversation was a blur. It was painful to sit there and listen to a long list of what our son could not do, but, we knew our 3-year-old son was depending on us to speak up for him.

When special education teachers disagree with the IEP team, the recourse is to write a Minority Report and have it attached to the IEP. When my husband and I disagreed with other IEP team members about placing our 3-year-old son in a special education preschool classroom instead of a community preschool, our recourse was to have many more IEP meetings. When we realized this was not resolving the disagreement, we filed for a Due Process Hearing. Thankfully, we were able to settle through a mediation session. The District agreed to our son attending a community preschool, paid his tuition, and provided a special education early-childhood teacher to collaborate weekly with the preschool staff.

Fast forward again, retired from 30 years of teaching (15 years as a special educator and 15 years as a general education teacher), I was looking for a new way to support students and parents. I went to work for Colorado's Parent Training and Information Center, PEAK Parent Center. PEAK has a national reputation for being a leader in providing parents with training and support so their children can be successfully included in schools and their community.

As the Educational Specialist at PEAK, I developed curriculum for trainings, facilitated workshops for parents and educators and also supervised Parent Advisors. Our Parent Advisors were awesome, experienced parents themselves and provided sound advice for parents over the telephone and sent them valuable resources. The one thing missing was the resources for the Parent Advisors to actually attend IEP meetings with families. This is the reality when a non-profit organization serves an entire state; the stretched-thin staff can only do so much.

During IEP meetings, parents are often asked questions they are not prepared to answer, or given information they do not understand. Seeing a need, I decided to pursue my private advocacy business for families, Collaborative Special Education Advocacy. I provide advice and resources to parents, and am also the guide by their side at IEP meetings, either in person, via Skype or FaceTime. As a parent of a young adult who received special education services, a special educator, classroom teacher, advocate for students, and adjunct university instructor, I have had many diverse experiences and perspectives to draw from. All of this has led me to continue to know the importance of taking action with and for others.

While researching material for this book, I was sometimes discouraged. I continued to observe parents frustrated when working with educators, trying to reach consensus about their children's needs and supports and services. I've been in IEP meetings where parents are not even reserved a spot to sit at the table and instead sit behind a large number of staff members. Guess how valuable that makes parents feel? I've heard the educators in the room give their reports one by one, describing the impact of the child's disability, their goals derived from their low expectations for the student - all without asking the parent for input. I've witnessed special education directors shut down a discussion and simply tell the parent, if they disagree to go ahead and file a complaint.

Of course, I would be remiss if I only gave examples of uncooperative behavior from the educators. I have also seen parents come to a meeting with a preplanned solution and not willing to accept any other options. I have heard parents describe how they can "get the teacher" by bringing up past experiences. And yes, I have seen parents refuse to listen to the staff and keep interjecting their ideas.

Though sometimes discouraged, I came to realize all the reasons to be optimistic. I have been in IEP meetings where there was genuine respect for each other; everyone was treated as an equal and valued member, and the students' best interests were always what decisions were based on. If this positive way of communicating with each other can happen in one school building, it is possible in each and every building across our country.

This book will teach you skills I have learned the hard way and truth be told, I am still learning. It is essentially about how to bridge the communication gaps and re-build trust between parents and school staff. You will learn how to be an active listener, the art of asking clarifying questions, the difference between what people say and what they really mean, how to ask for what your child needs, and specific problem solving strategies.

WHO THIS BOOK IS FOR

This book is written for parents of children with disabilities, who have a basic knowledge of special education laws and parental rights. The emphasis of the book is on effective communication skills and solution based thinking. This book will be helpful to you if you identify with any of the following examples:

- You're searching for ways to change a pattern of frustrating IEP meetings

- You want to develop more positive relationships with school staff

- You're struggling with how to effectively speak up for your child

- You're looking for creative options to having your child's needs met

- You want to know how to keep conversations focused on your child

WHAT THIS BOOK IS NOT ABOUT

This book does not discuss special education laws or your specific rights. This knowledge is important, but it goes beyond the scope of this book. I am not an attorney and cannot give legal advice. As an advocate, I am happy to talk with you about your specific situation. My contact information is in the CALL TO ACTION section of this introduction.

HOW TO USE THIS BOOK

This book is an inspirational guide for families, an educational tool to learn specific skills, and a practical resource guide to refer to on a regular basis. The first part of each chapter shares the WHY. After reading Simon Sinek's book, *Start with Why* I began to understand it is necessary to first get in touch with the why of what we do. Starting with the why helps us focus on the meaning, purpose, and passion. It is actually the why that determines what we do.

After we have reflected on the why, there are specific strategies of What Parents Can Do. In most chapters, scenarios are shared and then an analysis of the scenario is given to gain more insights. Each chapter ends with a Call to Action and Resources section for those interested in learning more. Also, watch for the Bonuses at the end of most chapters.

I am excited you took the action to buy this book. Thank you for wanting to learn more about being an effective advocate for your child. I always tell parents the 3Rs of Advocacy are: Relationships, Relationships, and Relationships. In the end, the most important goal is for your child to be happy, safe, and be a competent learner at school. Let's work together to get this done!

CALL TO ACTION:

Call me for a FREE phone consultation. Yes, this is your chance for a conversation about your child and my suggestions as an advocate. Call me at 208-340-5874 or email charmaine@cspeda.com to set up a time for us to talk. I will be happy to give you a free 30-minute phone consultation. If we are a good fit, you can consider working with me more to help you advocate for your child.

This is a Take and Go book. Take some new strategies and go forth and change things, not only for your child, for all the children that will come.

RESOURCES:

Simon Sinek's TED Talk   Use the link below to see the youtube video.

http://bit.ly/1fQ1qY0

Sinek, S. (2009). *Start with why: How great leaders inspire everyone to take action.* New York: Penguin

BONUS:

Get my free eBook, *IEP Meetings with Less Drama = Better Outcomes for Your Child.*

Use this link to download the free eBook www.cspeda.com/whats-new

I wrote the FREE eBook for you because I know what it is like to be a parent sitting at an IEP meeting, wondering how to make sense of everything being said and doubting if the meeting will really help your child. Inside the book, I share tips and strategies I've learned not only as a parent of a child with a disability but also as a retired special education teacher, general educator, and advocate. As you read the FREE eBook, I want you to know that your child's life has purpose. Their voice matters. Their dreams count. And they were born to make an impact. Go to www.cspeda.com/whats-new/ and download your free eBook. It is a great companion to the book you are reading now.

Chapter 1: Conflict and Collaborative Advocacy

Children are the priority. Change is the reality.

Collaboration is the strategy.

Judith Billings

I am often asked by parents if I had conflicts when my son was in school. In the Introduction I described our first disagreement with the district when my son was 3 years old. Yes, conflict happens and believe it or not, we do not want to eliminate all conflict. Conflict can actually lead to change and create new and helpful insights. There will be times when you chose to view conflicts as opportunities to help educate others. Hopefully, any conflicts you will have will lead to positive change not only for your child, but also for other students to come.

The Advocacy Institute and The Children's Law Clinic Duke University School of Law published, *Preparing for Special Education Mediation and Resolution Sessions: A Guide for Families and Advocates in November 2009*. In the guide, a study by researchers, Jeannie Lake and Bonnie Billingsley discuss the factors that contribute to parent-school conflict in special education. Eight categories of factors were discovered:

1. Different views about a child or a child's needs

Often, parents believe the educators view their child through a deficit-based model. The student's challenges are emphasized and the student is seen as a person to be fixed instead of a child with many gifts and strengths that can be built upon. Children can show certain abilities at school but not at home, or not at school but at home. This can leave parents and teachers with different conclusions on what the student is able to do.

2. Lack of shared knowledge

Often parents are frustrated trying to understand the special education system. Parents can be confused and unsure if they have the sufficient knowledge to make appropriate decisions about their child's educational supports and services. Educators give parents a written copy of their Procedural Safeguards, but that does not mean parents understand the special education process and their rights. Parents often do not even know what questions to ask so they can understand their role better.

3. Few service delivery options

Both educators and parents may notice there are few programming options available for students. There can also be challenges in trying to predict what the child will need in the future. Educators feel many parents are committed to only one solution and are unwilling to consider other suggestions. The quality of services in neighborhood schools, charter schools, and private schools can be a source of conflict.

4. Resource constraints

The lack of time, money, personnel, and materials all impact conflicts. There are situations where the lack of financial resources can pit parent of students without disabilities against parents of students with disabilities. Many times parents are fearful their child will not receive the education they deserve due to a lack of funding.

5. Devaluation of people

Everyone needs to be appreciated and validated. When parents do not feel they are equal partners with the school team it can cause disagreements. If parents believe they are just giving token input to a staff that has already made up their minds before hearing the parents' thoughts, trust will be shattered. When educators perceive that parents are questioning their skills and knowledge, they can become defensive and effective communication breaks down.

6. Power struggles

There are times when parents and school administrators engage in power plays to try and become the stronger voice during disagreements. Sometimes, either party may become passive-aggressive as a way to put the other party down. As parents, we have probably learned how engaging in power struggles with our children rarely resolves anything. Engaging in power struggles during IEP meetings takes an emotional toll on everyone and is very counterproductive.

7. Breakdown in communication

Conflicts can quickly escalate when people begin to talk at each other, interrupt each other, and refuse to try and understand the other person's point of view. A lack of ongoing conversations makes it difficult for parents and school staff to understand each other's perspectives.

8. Lack of trust

Relationships need to be nourished in order to build trust. When parents and school staff do not trust each other, it usually results in adversarial meetings and the outcome for the student is a no-win situation.

My decades of experience advocating for students have shown me that the two most common reasons for disputes between parents and educators are a breakdown in communication and a lack of trust. If you've been going to meeting after meeting and not seeing any acceptable results for your child, it is time to try something different. That is why I wrote this book for you. What has been tried in the past, has not worked. New techniques and strategies are needed to ensure your child will be the focus of discussions, to allow for more respectful communication and "out of the box" thinking at IEP meetings. I call this collaborative advocacy. Keep reading to see how this is different than traditional advocacy.

How is traditional Advocacy different than Collaborative Special Education advocacy?

Traditional advocacy is often seen as adversarial with hostile negotiations, which can lead to stalemates. Parents and/or educators may choose not to understand each other's perception, concede nothing and demand their solution be implemented. These actions are often accompanied by resentment and a complete lack of cooperation.

Many people grow up in a culture that treats conflict resolution as a competition. Unfortunately, if one side engages in this type of behavior, the other side believes they must react in the same way. It is common to see the people we disagree with as the enemy. However, this leads to heated arguing and in the end, it is the student who loses. In contrast, when everyone feels validated, respected and heard, transparent discussions can occur and a more collaborative approach can be used. So, let's learn a bit more about collaborative advocacy, an alternative way of speaking up for our children.

Collaborative Special Education advocacy is a process of:

• Listening for Understanding

• Communicating Effectively

• Creative Problem-Solving

Collaborative advocacy requires a shift in thinking. Instead of taking your own perspective and working forcefully to convince the other side you have the right answers, it means the hearing and understanding of both perspectives and exploring options that will work for the child. Adversarial confrontation is replaced by a cooperative look at the issues. The focus of all discussions will be the needs of the child, instead of adult egos. The goal of working together is to ensure a positive plan for your child's education will be written and implemented with fidelity.

Collaborative advocacy takes time on the front end, but will save time in the long run. A series of two or three meetings can make a significant difference with each party feeling heard and having enough time to engage in some creative problem solving. Parents may also realize much progress can be made between official meetings.

Collaboration will not just happen. It needs to be deliberate, structured, systematic, and ongoing. There are four levels of collaboration. The first level is building relationships. This can be done by honoring diverse cultures, open communication, listening first to understand and second to respond, giving appropriate thanks, and creating partnerships. Chapter 5 has more about building relationships.

The second level of collaboration is gathering information and resources. Families can share information about their child and what has worked and what has not worked in the past for their child at school. Educators and families can tap into strengths of each other. It is also helpful for parents and teachers to attend the same training workshops so they all receive the same information. This will probably mean having a conversation with the principal about opening up professional development classes or in-service workshops to all parents.

The third level of collaboration is developing collaborative plans of how teachers and parents will be equal partners. This is an action step so you want to identify the most important activities to accomplish, include deadlines when things will be accomplished and list who will be responsible for what.

The final level of collaboration is implementing the collaborative plan. Ongoing communication between parents and educators will be needed to figure out if the plan is working or if modifications need to be made.

Families need to have a responsibility to be involved in the implementation; otherwise, they will not be seen as equal partners.

I know you may feel skeptical about getting anywhere without having to fight for your child's rights. I know because I have felt that way, not only as a parent, but also, at times, when I advocated for students. There may be times you want to get even with someone who has wronged your child. However, there is a way to move forward in a more positive manner.

Do not get me wrong, there is a place for pursing your due process rights. When parents have exhausted cooperative avenues, there is a time and place for using more formal ways to resolve disputes.

This book focuses on more informal, alternative dispute resolution processes. You will learn the art of asking questions, the difference between what people say and what they really mean, how to ask for what your child needs, and specific problem solving strategies.

WHY:

Collaborative advocacy builds trust and encourages full participation by everyone. This positive type of advocacy incorporates different viewpoints and validates everyone's opinion. It can be a useful tool to minimize the stress of disagreements and resolve parent-school conflicts. This will also build a foundation for effective collaboration in the future.

WHAT PARENTS CAN DO:

1. To close the gap between different views of your child, describe a picture of your child, a balanced view of his strengths, interests, his challenges and needs. If possible, do this with the staff before the IEP meeting. You want both your vision and your concerns written in the IEP. Notice, I did not tell you to have your vision and concerns attached to the IEP. Attachments have a way of getting lost. This is your parent input and it is a required part of the IEP. Remember, you want each IEP to be one step closer to your vision, not away from it.

See the Bonuses at the end of this chapter for tools you can use to describe your child: Sample Student Profile and Blank Student Profile.

2. Do not let a lack of knowledge stand in your way. Learn additional information about the special education process and appropriate service options by reading credible websites, subscribing to newsletters, contacting your state Parent Training and Information Center, connecting with the Disability Rights organization, becoming a member of Council for Parent Attorneys and Advocates (COPAA), joining a local parent support group, and reading about best practices. See the Call to Action and Resources sections at the end of this chapter for specific website links you'll want to check out.

3. If you find yourself frustrated because there seems to only be few choices of where your child can receive their services/supports, paint a picture of what your bottom-line interests are and be open minded to considering a variety of solutions. You need to suspend judgment, find the common ground, and remember this is about your child. Read more about this in Chapter 6.

4. Individualized special education services can be expensive in terms of funding depending on the type of personnel needed to provide the supports and services. However, schools cannot use a lack of funds or staff availability as a reason not to provide a free and appropriate public education for your child.

5. There are times when parents and/or school staff feel devalued. If you are in a situation where you do not feel appreciated, do not react with strong emotions. Instead, go back to stating factual information and descriptions of what happened, all while keeping your tone polite.

6. Be aware when the conversation is turning into a power struggle. Remind yourself the meeting is about your child. Become quieter, let others vent if that is what they need to do.

7. When you feel communication breaking down, use the 3 Rs: Relax, Reflect, and Request. Relax: Take a few deep breaths, notice what part of

your body feels tense and when you exhale, see the tension leaving your body. Regroup: Give yourself a few seconds to remind yourself the focus is your child. Respond: Say what you have observed, state the feelings you are experiencing, what you want fulfilled, and make a specific request.

8. Here is a tip for developing trust: Ask for a pre-IEP meeting with a key person. This could be with the special education director, classroom teacher, or special educator. Meet somewhere off school grounds where it can be more relaxing and informal. Have a heart to heart conversation about the future you want for your child, the positive things currently happening that can be built on, and your desire for honest, open communication. Get a chance to truly listen to each other and appreciate where each person is coming from.

How to Resolve Top Eight Causes of

Special Education Conflicts

Causes of Conflict	Solution
1. Different views of child/needs	Describe a picture of your child as a balanced view of his strengths, interests, challenges and needs. Share the Student Profile. Have your input (vision & concerns) written in the IEP
2. Lack of shared knowledge	Learn what questions to ask and where to go for resources Ask to attend teacher in-service workshops

Causes of Conflict	Solution
3. Few service delivery options	Increase possibilities through creative problem solving.
4. Resource constraints	Evaluate how staff is currently allocated and consider changing some of their roles to better meet the needs of the students. Dialogue with other parent groups so they can share how they created more resources in their districts.
5. Devaluation of people	Do not react with strong emotions. Go back to stating factual information and descriptions of what happened while keeping your tone polite.
6. Power struggles	Remind yourself the meeting is about your child. Become quieter, let others vent if that is what they need to do.

Causes of Conflict	Solution
7. Break down in communication	Use the 3 Rs Relax, Reflect, and Request. Relax: Take a few deep breaths, notice what part of your body feels tense and when you exhale, see the tension leaving your body. Regroup: Give yourself a few seconds to remind yourself the focus is your child. Respond: Say what you have observed, the feelings you are experiencing, what needs you want fulfilled, and make a specific request.
8. Lack of trust.	Ask for a pre-IEP meeting with a key person. Have a heart to heart conversation about the future you want for your child, the positive things currently happening that can be built on, and your desire for honest, open communication Get a chance to truly listen to each other and appreciate where each person is coming from.

You may doubt your ability to pull off this new thing called collaborative special education advocacy. It can be challenging to change old ways of doing things. It can feel clumsy to say phrases that do not naturally flow out of your mouth. That is okay, you can learn and model a new way of communicating during IEP team meetings and other parent-teacher meetings. You'll get better at it with each conversation you have at school.

You do have the power to make change! Believe it, try the strategies outlined in this book, and remember, your child is counting on you to help advocate for him. You can do this!

CALL TO ACTION:

Go to www.cspeda.com/newsletters/ to sign up for my free monthly newsletter.

RESOURCES:

An abundance of resources for families and educators can be found at Wrightslaws website: wrightslaw.com

Find your state's Parent Training and Information Center: www.parentcenterhub.org/find-your-center/

Visit www.parentcenterhub.org/resources/ to access the Parent Center Resource Library.

Go to the Federal Department of Education's website

http://idea.ed.gov/ to better understand the federal law IDEA.

Visit www.copaa.org/ to access the Council of Parent Attorneys and Advocates' website.

Check out www.ndrn.org/index.php to access resources at the National Disability Rights Network's website.

BONUSES:

Bonus #1: Sample Student Profile (pages 18 – 20)

Bonus #2: Blank Student Profile. (pages 20 – 21)

Go to http://bit.ly/1kG1gY6 to print the Sample Student Profile. Here is the link for the Blank Student Profile http://bit.ly/1MUhIOQ

A student profile is an excellent way to share information about your child with the school staff. When parents explain what works and what does not work with their child, teachers will not have to waste precious teaching time trying to determine successful strategies to use. Parents can also identify their child's strengths, which will help the staff know what areas to build on so the student will be more successful. Here is a sample Student Profile. A blank Student Profile form follows.

Parents can use this same format, or create their own template for their child's profile.

Sample Student Profile

Student Name: David
      Age: 12   Grade: 7th

Strengths, Interests, Talents, Gifts:
David is empathetic, has a great sense of humor, is a great problem solver, is very motivated to learn more, loves to write lyrics to original songs, enjoys dancing, playing X box 360, keeping in touch with friends with his cell phone, emails, and on facebook. He loves performing skits and plays. David enjoys helping younger students learn new skills, reading picture books to younger students. He enjoys going to after school activities and being in the video club at the middle school.

Dislikes:
Loud noises, being left out, having people think he isn't capable of doing something, sitting up high in stadiums, not having choices, having his routine changed without advance notice.

Names of school friends:
Destiny, Kelli, Amanda, Michael, Ian, Kenny, and Zach.

Preferred learning style(s): Auditory, Visual, Tactile, Kinesthetic
David learns new skills by watching others first and then trying it himself.

Type of intelligence(s) strengths: Verbal/linguistic, Logical/mathematical, Visual/spatial, Musical/rhythmic, Bodily/kinesthetic, Interpersonal, Intrapersonal, Naturalist
David has strong visual and spatial skills. He has a strong sight word vocabulary and can remember how to get to places in the community. He has strong interpersonal skills: it is important for David to hang out with friends, he enjoys doing group activities.

Health Needs:
David can become dehydrated easily. He needs to drink water several times during the school day.

Effective Ways to Present Information:	Ineffective Ways to Present Information:
Hands-on activities, educational videos, visual aids	Lecture, requiring him to read a textbook
Effective Ways Student Can Demonstrate Learning:	**Ineffective Ways Student Can Demonstrate Learning:**
PowerPoint presentations, oral tests, projects	Written reports/tests
Effective Ways to Engage Student:	**Ineffective Ways to Engage Student:**
Relate to something David is interested in. Give him choices. Have him work with peers.	Dictating what he has to do without any choices.
Effective Accommodations/Modifications:	**Ineffective Accommodations/Modifications:**
Word Prediction software for his laptop, identify key concepts for him to be responsible for learning, recording pen to take notes, bringing special education supports to the general education classroom.	Alphasmart word processor, giving him curriculum that is unrelated to what the class is studying, being pulled out from the general education classrooms.

Effective Communication Strategies: He usually can understand what others are saying. If not, showing him a picture of the concept is helpful. David is persistent with repeating things, showing what he means so people can understand his "Down syndrome accent."	Ineffective Communication Strategies: Too much auditory input with little visual aids. Not giving him a chance to explain or show what he is thinking.
Effective Behavior Strategies: Allowing David to explain what happened, giving him choices of what else he could have done and letting him pick a solution to try.	Ineffective Behavior Strategies: No conversation about what happened, time out.

Blank Student Profile

Student Name:

    Age: Grade:

Strengths, Interests, Talents, Gifts:

Dislikes:

Names of school friends:

Preferred learning style(s): Auditory, Visual, Tactile, Kinesthetic

Type of intelligence(s) strengths: Verbal/linguistic, Logical/mathematical, Visual/spatial, Musical/rhythmic, Bodily/kinesthetic, Interpersonal, Intrapersonal, Naturalist

Health Needs:

Effective Ways to Present Information:	Ineffective Ways to Present Information:
Effective Ways Student Can Demonstrate Learning:	Ineffective Ways Student Can Demonstrate Learning:
Effective Ways to Engage Student:	Ineffective Ways to Engage Student:
Effective Accommodations/Modifications:	Ineffective Accommodations/Modifications:
Effective Communication Strategies:	Ineffective Communication Strategies:
Effective Behavior Strategies:	Ineffective Behavior Strategies:

Bonus #3: Visit http://bit.ly/1QOpfR0 to download the handout: How to Resolve Top Eight Causes of Special Education Conflicts

Conflict is growth trying to happen.

Dr. Harville Hendrix

Chapter 2: Listen and Ask Questions with Genuine Curiosity

Ask more questions.

Assume less.

Charmaine Thaner

Everyone sitting around the conference table felt the tension. The meeting was no longer a discussion, it had turned into everyone talking at the same time...sound familiar? Have you ever been in a meeting with teachers and you cannot wait for them to pause so you can jump in and let them know what you think? In your mind, you are rehearsing what you are going to say before the other person is even done talking. You have stopped listening to what they are saying and instead, you want to start saying what is on your mind. As Dr. Phil says, "How's that working for ya?" Probably not that well.

When we feel a strong sense of urgency to speak up, our listening drops dramatically. You will not change someone's mind by arguing with him or her. Instead, if you ask questions at school meetings, you can often learn how the school perceives your child's needs and what they are proposing to do to meet those needs.

WHY:

I love that phrase, "listen with curiosity." It brings up such a clearer picture of what we need to be practicing. This is a personal goal for me - to hear the other person's words, see their body language, and go beneath all of that to see if I can be a good detective and understand why they are saying what they're saying. That is when we can begin to really communicate on a level that is going to allow us to bring about collaborative change.

We know people in conflict must not only have the opportunity to speak, but to be heard. Once heard, everyone has a deeper understanding of the problem and potential ways it can be resolved.

Listening with curiosity helps give us insight into the other person's motivation and beliefs. This is important because we need to recognize where they are coming from. Each IEP team member has a role to play and that role is influenced by his or her motivation and beliefs.

When we listen with attention and respect, it shows people what they are saying is important. You may disagree with what they're saying, but when you show respect, it will go a long way in helping the conversations continue and be give and take.

Read on to see how you can change the way you react and really listen with curiosity.

WHAT PARENTS CAN DO:

1. Challenge yourself to set aside your opinion for a time in order to start to see the situation from someone else's perspective. The superintendent probably does not want the conflict to come up to his level, he is probably hoping the special education director takes care of the situation. The special education director may be thinking. "If I give into you, it will set a precedent and other parents will also start asking for more." The principal may be trying to figure out what role she plays in all of this. The special education teacher may be trying to come up with a way to agree with you

and not "rock the boat" at the same time. Know that their specific roles play a part in the multiple perspectives being played out at the meeting.

2. Notice both the emotion and what the speaker is saying. Do this without thinking of what you are going to say next. That is the key, to listen, without thinking of what you're going to say next.

3. While listening, do not think about who is right. This can be another tricky one. Leave the, "I'm right, you're wrong" attitude at the door.

4. Keep focused on the conversation. When your mind starts going into blah, blah, blah thinking mode you know you need to call yourself back and get back focused on the conversation.

5. Bring someone else who can take notes for you, it makes it easier to listen better. Yes, bring a partner, friend, spouse, neighbor, relative, someone, not only to be a note taker, but for moral support. That is important; IEP meetings can be very emotional and you need to feel supported when you're looking at a large group of other people from the school.

6. Remember, your face and posture show if you are listening or not. Faking it is not allowed. If you need to, remind yourself that decisions will be made that have a big impact on your child. Stay in the conversation!

7. As much as staying in the conversation is important, allow for silences. This is true especially after you ask a question. Do not fill up the empty air space with more comments from you. There are times when having a lull in the conversation can be beneficial. You want the person to answer your question, and if you keep talking after asking a question, you take them off the hook to respond.

8. Listen without interrupting and making judgments. I have had to apologize more than once for interrupting during a meeting. I can now catch myself more, which is a good thing. I have noticed when one person interrupts and people allow that, it seems to give everyone in the room

permission to interrupt when they feel the urge. Needless, to say, this leads to a very unproductive meeting.

One of my personal and professional goals is to ask more questions and presume less. When I was teaching, I learned asking questions was very helpful. On one occasion, I saw a student dumping all the dirt out of his flowerpot where he just planted his lima bean. Instead of saying , "Stop dumping out that dirt." I asked him, "What are you doing?" Guess what I found out? The student was dumping the dirt out to find his lunch money - he had buried it to make sure it was safe. My first assumption was he was trying to make a mess - good thing I asked a question and learned what he was really trying to do.

An important listening tool is to ask questions. On the next few pages there are several examples of clarifying and probing questions. However, these questioning techniques will not be effective if you only go through the motions, or ask the questions with sarcasm. They must be asked with the true intent of gaining a better understanding of where the person is coming from.

CLARIFYING QUESTION: "I would like to ask a few questions to see if I understand the facts presented today."

WHY:

Discussions may have missing information or be unclear. Clarifying this will lead to a better understanding of the other person's perspective. Sometimes the message sent is not heard the way it was intended and misunderstandings can happen. When clarifying questions are asked, people are more likely to understand each other better, a give and take environment is created, and more back and forth conversations will happen.

WHAT PARENTS CAN DO:

1. Be clear on the facts before moving forward.

2. Seek to fully understand what the other person is expressing. There may be times when it seems risky and uncomfortable to set aside our views, even for a short time, in order to see the other person's perspective.

3. Repeat back to them, in their words what you heard them say.

SCENARIO:

Clarifying question: "Could I ask a few questions to see if I understand the facts presented today?"

Parent:

- Is Ben completing more morning or afternoon assignments?

- Does Ben ask for help from a peer or the teacher when he does not understand the task?

- Is Ben using the additional time he is given to complete assignments?

ANALYSIS:

When a list of facts is stated, it can sound threatening or lecturing. Whenever possible, ask a question instead. Asking questions allows the other person a chance to participate, listen, and either accept it or correct it. Asking questions also allows everyone to start with agreed upon facts before you begin to look for solutions.

****

CLARIFYING STATEMENT: Let me get back to you.

WHY:

You want to be clear about what decision is most appropriate. Give yourself permission to take some time to think over what would be the correct decision.

WHAT PARENTS CAN DO:

1. Take time before making decisions.

2. Talk over the option(s) presented with someone else and get their feedback.

SCENARIO:

Parent:

Thank you for helping me understand the information. I would like to talk with my husband and explain it to him. Let me get back to you by tomorrow afternoon and then we can discuss next steps."

ANALYSIS:

If you are like many parents, it is a good idea to take at least 24 hours to "sleep on" a conversation before making a final decision. If you try and make a decision on the spot, you might yield to the psychological pressure to be nice and give in.

****

CLARIFYING QUESTION: Could you show me some examples?

WHY:

Increase your understanding by asking for examples.

WHAT PARENTS CAN DO:

1. Show a genuine desire to understand.

2. If once you see the examples you still have questions, ask for more clarification.

3. Remember, there is no such thing as a stupid question!

SCENARIO:

General Education Teacher:

"Thank you for coming to Ethan's parent-teacher conference. We sent his report card home yesterday so you could get a chance to look at it beforehand. You can see he is doing well in all of his subjects except for written language. He continues to struggle to write supporting details and include a conclusion."

Parent:

"Yes, we are pleased with his progress, and are also concerned with the grade he got for Writing. We do have him write thank you letters to his grandparents when he receives gifts from them. We think he does a good job with those. I guess we are not sure what you mean about writing supporting details and a conclusion. He doesn't bring home much of his schoolwork. Could you show us some examples of writing he does in class?

General Education Teacher:

"Yes, I would be happy to. Here is his writing folder with some samples of his writing. This story begins with him talking about going on a family camping trip. He said he had a lot of fun, but doesn't describe what was fun about the trip. He wrote that you cooked all your meals on the campfire. It would help the reader to know more details - what was cooked, what meals he liked best, if it was easy or hard to cook on a campfire. You can also see he just stops writing without having a real ending."

Parent:

"What does he have to do to become a better writer?" Could you show me some examples of what other students in his class are writing?"

General Education Teacher:

"Sure, here is an anchor writing sample - which means an example of what we expect students in Ethan's grade to be writing. The example shows four paragraphs with a beginning sentence, followed by at least three details. At the end of the story, there is a conclusion that summarizes what happened in the story."

Parent:

"So, Ethan should be doing all of that in every story he writes?"

General Education Teacher:

"No, we look at what his writing goal is on his IEP. We are expecting him to write a three-paragraph story with two details in each paragraph and a conclusion by this time in the school year. I have talked with the special education teacher about trying a different way of helping him with his written language. She thinks a more visual outline of what needs to be included in his stories may help him be more successful."

Parent:

Well, I am so glad we came tonight for the conference. Now I understand so much better what he has been doing and what we want him to do. I am glad the special education teacher has another idea to try. I think when we have him write thank you notes at home we will tell him he has to say at least three things he likes about the gift."

General Education Teacher:

"Yes, that is a terrific idea. Thanks so much for supporting what Ethan is learning at school. I am looking forward to the progress he will make this next quarter."

ANALYSIS:

The parents not only asked to see an example of their son's writing, but they also continued asking questions until they understood what the grade level expectations were and specifically what Ethan was supposed to be doing according to his IEP.

Side note: Did you see how the parent-teacher conference was with the general education teacher? This reinforces the fact that Ethan is one of her students, he is not the special education teacher's student.

****

Probing Question: What would it take to ...?

WHY:

By asking probing questions it allows everyone to think more deeply about the issues. You will gather more useful information and learn more. Probing questions are more open-ended and help you find out the other person's opinion or values. Being direct and getting to the bottom line can help resolve the problem faster.

WHAT PARENTS CAN DO:

1. Give an idea and ask what would need to happen to implement that idea.

2. Once you ask a question, you need to be quiet and let the other person answer without your "yabbit" (yes, but) knee jerk response.

SCENARIO:

Parent:

"We have been talking about our shared concerns with Jacob using the locker room without any adult supervision. What would it take to have the

PE teacher be in his glass enclosed office, which is in the locker room, before and after the PE class?"

Counselor:

"Well, I can't dictate to the PE teacher what he has to do before and after his classes."

Parent:

"We have talked many times about making sure Jacob is not bullied while he is in the locker room. What would it take to have the PE teacher in his office before and after Jacob's PE class?"

Counselor:

"I agree we don't want Jacob bullied. I suppose we could have a conversation with the PE teacher and the principal to see how feasible your suggestion would be."

Parent:

"Great. When can that meeting be arranged?"

Counselor:

"The principal is out of the building today, but I can check with him tomorrow and see when we can meet with the PE teacher."

Parent:

"Thank you. I will be expecting a call or email from you after school tomorrow."

ANALYSIS:

The parent begins with the shared concerns he and the counselor agree on. When you start with what has already been discussed and agreed to, the conversation is able to move forward. The parent made a reasonable suggestion and did not get sidetracked by the counselor's first remark. The key players (counselor, parent, principal and PE teacher) will meet where the parent will again ask, "What would it take to...?" Once again, there is accountability for when the parent will be notified about the upcoming meeting.

****

PROBING QUESTION: "Can you help me understand why that was done?"

WHY:

Understand the other person's point of view

WHAT PARENTS CAN DO:

Dig deeper to find out the whole story

SCENARIO:

Parent:

"We noticed when we came to the music program last night that Sophia was standing off to the side with a para-educator and was not given an instrument to play like all her classmates were. Can you help me understand why that was done?"

General Education Teacher:

"I talked to the Music teacher and we were both concerned that Sophia might not sing the correct words or play the instrument at the correct time. We didn't want to embarrass her."

Parent:

"What was the reason she was standing off away from the group?"

General Education Teacher:

"I'm not sure, maybe the para-educator thought that was a better place for her."

Parent:

"Why was the para-educator standing next to her throughout the performance?"

General Education Teacher:

"I think the Music teacher wanted to make sure Sophia had support."

Parent:

"Did you notice if any of Sophia's classmates were not singing the correct words, or playing their instrument at the correct time?"

General Education Teacher:

Laughing, "Well yes, that is pretty normal with this age group of kids."

Parent:

"I appreciate that you and the Music teacher did not want Sophia to be embarrassed and to be supported. My husband and I agree with that. You probably remember the conversation you and I had with Sophia when she talked about feeling dumb and worried other kids were laughing at her when a para-educator is right next to her. We would like to set up a meeting with you, the Music teacher, Sophia and myself to talk about how she can be supported using natural supports and how she can have the same opportunities as her friends to have fun together and know it is okay if she forgets some words or forgets to play her instrument at the exact right time. When can that meeting happen?"

General Education Teacher:

"Well, the Music teacher and I both have a common planning time on Wednesdays after lunch. Could we meet next Wednesday at twelve-thirty?

Parent:

"Next Wednesday at twelve-thirty will be perfect. Thanks for being willing to discuss how Sophia can use natural supports and actively participate in all her classes."

ANALYSIS:

The parent started with an objective observation she made. The teacher will be less defensive when non-judgmental facts are stated. The mother only asked one question at a time and then paused for the teacher to answer. The parent did not argue each point with the teacher. Instead she pointed out the common ground they shared - not to embarrass Sophia and to make sure she was supported. The goal of this conversation is to understand the other person's point of view - not to have a debate. The mother shared a previous discussion where Sophia talked about her feelings of a para-educator being by her and their families' goals to have Sophia use natural supports and share the same opportunities as her friends. The parent reiterated the purpose of the meeting and the specific day and time for the meeting.

****

PROBING QUESTION: What are your concerns?

WHY:

Understand the other person's point of view.

WHAT PARENTS CAN DO:

Stay interested in finding out more about where others are coming from.

SCENARIO:

Parent:

"I want to make sure my wife and I understand your point of view. What are your concerns with having Logan included in his general education classroom?

Principal:

"I want every student in our building to be successful and make gains each year. In fact, I am responsible for every student in this building. When I look at where Logan is functioning in math and language arts and how wide the gap is between him and his peers I don't see how we can expect a classroom teacher to stop what she is doing with other students and focus on Logan. We have special education teachers who have the specific training and experience in working with students like Logan. I don't understand why you wouldn't want Logan to be in a small group with a special education teacher so he can learn at his level."

Parent:

Thank you for your honesty. Is this summary of your concerns correct?

• how having Logan included in his general education classroom will impact other students and their learning

• how a classroom teacher can address Logan's learning needs while also teaching the other students in the room

• why do we want Logan included when there are special education teachers and special education classrooms in the building

Principal:

Yes, I think that is an accurate summary of my concerns. We all care about Logan and want him succeed, but you have to remember we have 427 other students in this building.

Parent:

It seems it would be helpful if we can talk more with you about the Why and How of inclusion. Do you have time to continue this discussion now?

Principal:

I do have another appointment in 15 minutes. Can we schedule another time to meet? You can just check with my secretary and she can get you on my calendar.

Parent:

"That will work. I also wanted to leave a copy of this DVD that explains the benefits of inclusion for students with and without disabilities. It also shows several classrooms and how co-teaching and Universal Design for Learning can make inclusive education a positive experience for students and teachers. It addresses your concerns and I would be interested in your reaction to it. Thank you for your time and your commitment to all the students in your building."

ANALYSIS:

The parent shows a genuine interest in the principal's concerns. This helps the principal know that his opinion counts. The parent thanked the principal for his honesty, summarized his concerns and asked if it was accurate. The parent identified two How concerns and one Why concern from the principal's perspective. This shows the principal is unclear on why the parents are requesting inclusive education for their son. The principal is also thinking of how this can really be successfully implemented in classrooms without negatively impacting other students.

The parent decided to leave a DVD with the principal to view, knowing that it is very beneficial for educators to see what inclusive education looks like.

The examples above are to help you understand how to use clarifying and probing questions when having discussions, parent-teacher conferences, IEP meetings, and in many other situations.

Remember: Your tone of voice when asking questions is critical. If you shout the question, use a judgmental or sarcastic tone of voice you will be right back in the arguing mode. You do not want this to happen. So, ask your questions in a calm manner. Be genuine about wanting to understand the other person's point of view. This will help resolve conflicts and get you on the road to helping your child be safe, successful, and happy.

Tip: Before the meeting: Talk with the person who will be leading the meeting and ask if they agree that asking clarifying and probing questions before making judgments can create more positive results. If they agree, ask if a list of sample questions can be posted in the conference room for everyone to see and use during the meeting.

CALL TO ACTION:

Role-play with a trusted family member or friend some of the scenarios that you think will likely happen at your next IEP meeting. When you practice what to say in certain situations, you will be more confident in the meeting.

RESOURCES:

Sound expert, Julian Treasure shares *5 Ways to Listen Better*, to other people and to the world around you. To view the video, go to:

http://bit.ly/1n854wJ

Visit http://bit.ly/1kG2eUb to see a great Infographic on questioning

Movie and TV clips about asking questions:

http://bit.ly/1WZWpSH

BONUS:

Visit http://bit.ly/1lvFiag to download more examples of Clarifying/Probing Questions and Comments.

When you act upon and make changes as a result of what you learn,

your child reaps the benefits.

Charmaine Thaner

Chapter 3: How to Listen With Your Eyes

Body language is words heard with the eyes.

Bodies reflect fear, boredom, interest, repulsion, openness,

attraction, caring, hatred.

Bodies will speak to us,

if we will carefully listen with our eyes.

Gerry Spence

What people are saying can be very different from what they are thinking or feeling. When we communicate with others, we need to be aware of the importance of having our body language and tone of voice match our words, or we will send confusing messages. We probably all have experienced asking a friend how they are, hearing them say "fine", but knowing by the scowl on their face and disgusted tone, that they are definitely not feeling fine. If you do not have the communication skills to get to the real meaning behind your friend's words it can lead to frustration for both of you.

Nonverbal communication is as important as verbal communication. Many researchers are finding that body language accounts for between 50 and 80% of our communication.

Note: We also need to be aware of cultural differences in the meanings of body language. Shaking hands, giving the Okay sign or thumbs up do not necessarily mean the same thing in other cultures as they do in Western culture.

Body Language, Facial Expressions, and Voice

WHY:

When you become more skilled at reading body language you can learn how people truly feel, what they really mean and ultimately understand others better. Being able to read others allows you to communicate more effectively. This can also boost your persuasion powers and win people's trust.

When you practice being able to tell when there is a contradiction between what a person is saying and what their body language is saying, you will have more insight into what they are thinking on an emotional level.

Understanding, interpreting, and controlling your own body language are key skills which can make a difference in how successful you are when talking with others.

WHAT PARENTS CAN DO:

1. One way to discover what the body language of someone else is, is to copy his or her body language and then ask how you are feeling when you take on the other person's body language.

2. Remember, while you may be looking for meaning in others' body language, chances are they are also evaluating your body language. The signals you send will probably influence how people perceive you.

3. Be aware of a speaker's body language: facial expressions, body language, tone of voice and gestures. It is important to note that just one body cue is not a reliable indicator. Body language needs to be interpreted in context of the person's tone of voice and signs being given by the whole body. In order to understand body language, people need to look for several consistent signals. Also, be aware that some people have learned to "fake" body language signals to confuse the other party. Here are some common body cues and what they may mean if they are seen in combination with similar signals:

<u>Raising one eyebrow/tilting head to one angle:</u> according to Patti Wood, author of *Snap: Making the Most of First Impressions, Body Language, and Charisma*, this may mean the person is not being honest - what he says does not match what he feels.

<u>Rolling the eyes:</u> an upward roll of the eyes can mean the person is frustrated or exasperated.

<u>Staring and blinking:</u> if you see someone staring at the ceiling and blinking rapidly it may mean they are thinking about the point being made.

<u>Clasping hands behind the back:</u> can be a symbol of confidence, power, or authority

<u>Open palms, or facing upwards:</u> can signify honesty, submissiveness and cooperation.

<u>Fingers together with the hand pointing upwards:</u> it can suggest thought, making connections and examining ideas.

<u>Clenched hands:</u> usually a sign of anxiety or an attempt to calm the thoughts and to hold them in.

<u>Leaning in:</u> person is interested in the conversation

<u>Tapping feet:</u> a lack of confidence in what is being said.

<u>Starting to rub face, neck, or legs:</u> may mean the person is uncomfortable with the topic. Tony Reiman, author of *The Body Language of Dating*, points out other cues when people are uncertain: blinking their eyes a lot, shrugging the shoulders, and shifting their weight from side to side.

<u>Supporting chin with a thumb, while one finger rests over the lip:</u> can indicate serious consideration, holding back opinions, and evaluating clearly.

<u>Touching jewelry:</u> usually is a sign of discomfort, fear, and nervousness. Person may be afraid of impending loss or attack.

<u>A genuine smile:</u> may be accompanied by a lifting of the body up, reaching out to the other person, can mean the person is truly happy.

<u>A tight smile that quickly fades:</u> this often means the person is not really happy.

<u>Stopping the conversation and changing the topic</u>: the person does not want to do something. This may also be shown when a person uses short, to the point sentences.

4. Each person has his or her own unique body language signals and there might be a different underlying cause from the one you are thinking. This is especially true when people have different past experiences. This is why it is important to check that your interpretation of someone else's body language is correct.

5. Pay full attention to speaker: listen with your ears and eyes. Look for feelings. Learn to read facial expressions and other body language. Careful observation is necessary to understand body language.

6. Pay attention to your voice: by varying your tone, some high and some low pitches, this will help you be more compelling and engaging, smile while talking so you are more friendly and responsive, speak a little faster and the others will feel your excitement and you can be seen as competent and smart, and take deep breaths to relax and calm your voice down

Choosing Your Words

WHY:

Increase understandings, better discuss issues and manage our conflicts.

WHAT PARENTS CAN DO:

1. Be brief, succinct, and organized. Organize your thoughts beforehand and practice saying them, and you will be more successful getting what your child needs.

2. Thinking about going to your next IEP meeting may bring up so many issues you want to make sure get addressed. In order to not start rambling and make people wonder what point you are trying to make, take some time to prepare.

3. At least several days before the meeting, make a list of what you want to cover during the meeting. It will be helpful to share this with the staff ahead of time so they know what your priorities are for the meeting.

4. Next to each issue, make a list of facts about it, questions you can ask during the meeting (see Chapter 4), and space for writing the district's response. Taking time to reflect on your thoughts and feelings will help you more clearly express your thoughts. See the Bonus with a sample form you can use to track the issues you want discussed at the IEP meeting.

5. Make sure you always include some compliments you can give the staff. Just as we parents like to hear positive things about our children, the staff need to hear what we appreciate about their work with students.

6. Tailor your message to align with the person's thinking style and mood at the time. If the person is a visual learner you can use phrases such as: How do you see the situation? or What is your viewpoint? When talking with a person that is more of an auditory thinker, use phrases such as: I hear what you are saying. or I would like to hear what you have to say. Some people are more kinesthetic thinkers. With these people you can choose phrases, such as: I know how you feel. or Let's jump right in.

CALL TO ACTION:

Pick one new book to read from, What's on my Bookshelf: http://www.cspeda.com/resources/whats-on-my-bookshelf/

RESOURCES:

Visit http://bit.ly/1v4YQQL for several interesting articles about body language.

BONUS:

You can use the sample form when you are preparing for a meeting with school staff. It could be used for an IEP meeting, Parent - Teacher conferences, a meeting with the principal, etc.

Visit http://bit.ly/1HYRsCJ to download the form for Exploring Issues.

Sample Form for Exploring Issues

Issue	Facts	Questions to Ask	District's Response

Our verbal and nonverbal responses to others can either continue the conversation or shut it down.

Charmaine Thaner

Chapter 4: Know What to Say When

Texting is a brilliant way to miscommunicate

how you feel,

and misinterpret what other people mean.

Lessonslearnedinlife.com

There will be many times when it is helpful to know how to follow up after conversations, how to keep everyone's focus on your child and/or, emphasize what is appropriate for your child. On the next few pages are four examples of useful conversation starters, what to do, a short scenario, and an analysis that explains why you say what and when to say it.

FOLLOW-UP TO CONVERSATION: Please correct me if I'm wrong.

WHY:

You have probably heard this before, If it is not in writing, it did not happen. Take the time to verify all verbal conversations with a written email or letter so there is no, He said - She said later on.

WHAT PARENTS CAN DO:

1. Follow up all phone calls or other verbal conversations with an email to confirm or correct your understanding of what was said.

2. Make sure when writing an email, you include everyone involved in the issue and all the decision makers.

3. Document, document, document.

Example of Follow-Up Email

Dear Ms. Jones,

Thank you for spending time on the phone with me this morning as we discussed Zach's need for assistive technology (AT). I understood that:

• The district's AT team will complete an evaluation of Zach's needs by Oct. 1st.

• As part of the evaluation, I will have a conversation with the AT team to give the parent perspective and they will also talk with Zach about what he thinks will be most helpful.

• The IEP team will meet on Oct. 15th to amend the IEP in order to include Zach's AT needs and necessary devices and supports.

Please correct me, by the end of the week (Sept. 8th), if I'm wrong with my summary of our conversation. Otherwise, the list above of the tasks to be done, by whom, and by when, will be what we have agreed to.

Thank you again for your time. I know Zach is excited about how assistive technology can help him be more successful. I am glad we are collaborating and look forward to positive outcomes.

Sincerely,

Catherine Monroe

ANALYSIS:

You want to clarify what was verbally agreed to so there are no future confusions. Notice the email was short and sweet. The main ideas of the conversation were written in bullet points to keep it more concise. Specific actions, who will do it and by when, were included in the points to aid with a clear understanding and ensure accountability.

You gave the person a chance to correct any misunderstandings, again, with a deadline for when that is to happen. You gave them notice, stating if there are no corrections by the date given, the expectation of what will happen is what you have listed.

Another important point to note: In the example, the mother specifically mentioned Zach by name throughout the email. This is to remind everyone reading the email that the focus is on Zach. Just as it should be.

The email began and ended with a sentence of thanks. You want to model the importance of separating the person from the problem. A note of appreciation allows the receiver of the email to know this is not about you versus them. Instead, this is about Zach and his assistive technology needs.

****

FOCUS CONSERVATION: Focus on your child's *needs*, not what you *want*.

WHY:

Want is a four-letter word you do not want to use in a meeting. The law does not care what you want for your child. Your child's education is based on what he needs. Keep the focus on your child's needs. Another four-letter word to avoid using is, best. Your child is only entitled to what is appropriate, not the best.

WHAT PARENTS CAN DO:

1. Eliminate the word want from your vocabulary. Your child's services and supports are based on her unique needs, not what you want. The school has to meet your child's needs, not your wants. Start substituting the word need for want. Say, "My child needs to be with same-aged peers so he can learn appropriate social skills." Do not say, "I want my child included!"

2. Attorney Gary Mayerson, in his book, *How to Comprise With Your School District Without Comprising Your Child*, suggests parents can show evidence of your child's needs with evaluations, data, progress reports, anecdotal evidence, and effective advocacy at IEP meetings.

3. Practice saying what your child needs and why they need it, before the meeting. You can even role-play this with a friend. Have your friend help you rehearse what to say and how to respond to possible questions.

4. Another word to eliminate from your vocabulary is best. The federal special education law does not say your child will receive what is best for her. Your child is only entitled to having her unique needs met. Substitute the word appropriate for the word best. Get in the habit of doing this.

SCENARIO:

Parent:

I appreciate you scheduling time to meet with my husband and me. We are proud of the academic gains Maria has made this semester. The core teachers have done an excellent job having her engaged in all the class learning activities, implementing the accommodations written in her IEP, and communicating her progress with us.

Special educator:

Well, that is great to hear! I have enjoyed co-teaching in her Language Arts and Science classes.

Parent:

We have noticed her grades in her elective classes have really taken a nosedive this semester. Maria has told us she feels overwhelmed in her Spanish and Technology classes trying to keep up with all the assignments that are due and having enough time to finish the tests.

Special educator:

Hmm, this is the first I have heard about this. I do have a lot of students on my caseload and do not have a planning period this year. I do my best to keep up with how students are doing. I do put more of a priority on the academic classes and touching base with those teachers.

Parent:

Our concern is having Maria's needs met. The IEP team did a terrific job describing her strengths, how her disability impacts her learning, and what her unique needs are. Do you know if her elective teachers have had a chance to read her IEP? Maria said she does not receive copies of her elective teachers' lecture notes beforehand and is not being given extra time for the tests in these two classes.

Special educator:

Well, all of our middle school teachers are very busy planning their lessons, grading homework and assessments when they are not teaching. I do send out emails at the beginning of the year letting teachers know the IEPs are in the file cabinet in my room. I am not sure if each and every teacher reads IEPs for every student they have.

Parent:

Our concern is having Maria's needs met. What do you think would be the most appropriate way to let her Spanish and Technology teachers know what is written in her IEP?

Special educator:

I hope you know how much we all care about Maria. I can set up a time to meet with each one of her elective teachers and go over the IEP with them. The other thing I did for her academic teachers was give each of them a summary of the IEP and made sure they understood her learning strengths, her goals and accommodations. I can also share this with her elective teachers.

Parent:

That sounds like an excellent plan. Will you be able to meet with those two teachers by the end of next week?

Special educator:

Yes, I will set those meetings up right away and give you a call to let you know how they went.

Parent:

Great! Thanks again for your time today.

ANALYSIS:

The parent began the conversation with specific things teachers are doing well. Take advantage of every opportunity to stress the positive. Next, the parent stated specific concerns in two of Maria's classes. The conversation did not get side tracked by other issues. The parent kept coming back to the main concern - how to get Maria's needs met. When the special educator came up with a plan, the parent expressed appreciation. Notice, when the other person comes up with a plan they will have more ownership in getting it done. A deadline of the end of next week was given for the meeting to occur and the special educator committed to calling the parent after the meeting.

****

REPHRASING CONVERSATION: I must not be explaining myself clearly. What I am trying to say is...

WHY:

You need to make sure both parties are on the same page. Without this shared understanding, you can both be going off on tangents that are not helpful.

WHAT PARENTS CAN DO:

1. Rephrase what you have said, give an example, or show a written sample of what you are talking about.

2. When thinking of how to make persuasive points during a discussion, it can be helpful to have sentence frames you can use. Ross, Fisher, & Frey, 2009 offer these examples.

The evidence I use to support _____ is _____.

I believe _____(statement) because _____(justification).

I know that _____ is _____ because _____.

Based on _____ I think _____.

Based on _____ my hypothesis is _____.

SCENARIO:

Parent:

My son's IEP says the staff working with him will follow the prompt guidelines - from just needing a verbal reminder to actually helping him do the task with hand-over-hand guidance. I am not sure if the new staff working with him this year are familiar with all of the different types of prompts that work well with Devon and when to use which prompt. I have brought a written description of the prompt guidelines teachers have successfully used in the past. I am requesting this be included in his IEP so we are all working together.

Special educator:

Thanks for sharing the prompt guidelines. I think these will be helpful for many of the staff. Let's set up a time to formally amend the IEP so these guidelines are included. Can you check on your calendar and let me know when you could come to the school for a short meeting.

Parent:

Thanks, I didn't know about amending the IEP. I will send you an email tomorrow letting you know some good days and times for me. Thanks for all of your help.

ANALYSIS:

The parent refers to what is written in the IEP as a starting point. The parent does not accuse staff of not knowing what they are doing. Instead, the parent shows understanding that it can be challenging for new staff to know exactly what the prompt guidelines are for this particular student. Next, the parent shares a written description of the guidelines to provide more clarity. And lastly, the request is made to include the prompt guidelines in the IEP - because we all know, if it is not written in the IEP it does not exist or have to be followed.

****

CHILD-FOCUSED CONVERSATION: What is most important right now is ...

WHY:

Resolving the problem will only happen when everyone remembers the child is the center of the discussion.

WHAT PARENTS CAN DO:

1. It is easy to get sidetracked when having discussions. Some parents bring a photograph of their child and place it in the middle of the table. This can be a visual reminder of whom the meeting is about.

2. You need to suspend judgment, find the common ground, and remember this about your child.

3. Keep the conversation focused on your child. It is not about how many other students the teacher has, the school or district budget, or how the school always does things.

SCENARIO:

Parent:

What is most important right now is having alternative assessments in place so Emma can show us what she knows and what she is able to do.

Special Education Teacher:

Yes, we have tried traditional tests and we know Emma is not very successful with those. But, we only have so much time to prepare alternatives for each class she is taking. We ask the general education teachers for their lesson plans a week ahead of time and rarely get them. We can only do so much when we don't know the date of classroom tests and the material it is going to cover.

Parent:

I agree the tests teachers use with other students don't show us an accurate picture of what Emma understands and can do. We want to focus on alternative assessments that are appropriate and tap into her strengths. She is really motivated when she can use her laptop and make a presentation to the class. Her English teacher has allowed her to do this instead of taking the pencil/paper tests. Is there a way other teachers can offer this option to her?

Special Education Teacher:

I didn't know her English teacher was doing that. I could ask him to show Emma's other teachers how he grades her presentations and uses it to determine what she has learned. We will have some time on Wednesday during our in-service day to do this.

Parent:

Sounds like a plan! I look forward to hearing from you after the in-service day. I will also talk to Emma about her teachers working together to come up with some ways for her to show what she knows. I am sure Emma will be excited.

ANALYSIS:

The parent begins the conversation with a short, clear statement that is focused on what her daughter needs. She does not let herself be sidetracked by the school's problems the teacher brings up. When she has the opportunity to agree with the teacher she does, "I agree the tests teachers use with other students don't show us an accurate picture of what Emma understands and can do..." The conversation will be more positive and the teacher will be more willing to continue talking with the parent when there are some points of agreement. The parent gives an example of what another teacher is using that is working with her daughter. Teachers will often follow the advice of another teacher and be more agreeable to trying what a colleague has found to be successful.

Near the end of the conversation, the parent asks for a timeline when the meeting with all her daughter's teachers will occur. It is important to have a date for when things will happen. The teacher volunteered to email the parent after the in-service meeting. If the teacher had not offered a way to communicate the results of the meeting, it would be important for the parent to ask for it.

Compassionate Communication

Do you ever feel frustrated, confused, and/or at a loss for words during conversations? Or do you know what you want to say but are unsure how to phrase your request? Join the crowd-we've all experienced these situations!

Sometimes when we feel criticized, blamed or judged, it is easy for us to respond in the same way. However, Dr. Marshall B. Rosenberg, founder of the Center for Non-Violent Communication, developed a way of responding which leads to more communicating. Dr. Rosenberg suggests four steps, I have adapted his model by adding a positive statement at the beginning and end of the process.

This communication strategy goes beyond "I messages" and provides a better framework for conversations when there are some concerns. First, you share an objective observation about the issue. Then you share a feeling about a need that is not being met. Finally, you request a specific action. And it is most effective to sandwich these comments between beginning and ending positive statements that express appreciation and gratitude.

 Here is an example of a parent speaking to her son's third grade teacher:

I want to thank you for your commitment to seeing all students as competent learners. I've noticed that when John is taken to the resource room for reading help, he comes home saying he's dumb and he hates school. I feel concerned because John's need to feel that he's really part of a third grade class is not being met. It's having a negative impact on his overall school experience. What would it take to provide additional reading instruction to John in his third grade classroom? I really appreciate all you do to ensure John's inclusion and success in third grade.

WHY:

Compassionate communication lets us connect with each other in a more positive way. It helps us be more assertive, instead of aggressive in our conversations. We also need to hear these four pieces of information from others: what the person observes, feels, needs, and requests. It is also important to hear the unspoken messages that may be communicated by another's tone of voice, body language, etc. Improvements in our communication can increase trust and enhance relationships, generating better outcomes for all!

WHAT PARENTS CAN DO:

1. Make a positive statement. Beginning with something positive helps to diffuse a potentially negative situation. Start the conversation with something you appreciate about the other person or something you are thankful that they have done.

2. Describe an observation, making no judgments. Take a step back and as if you are watching the situation from afar, describe what you see. Do so in very objective terms, no judgments allowed.

3. Share your feelings about what you have observed. Even when objectively describing a situation, you will have certain emotions attached to that event or conversation. It is important to be able to accurately describe the feelings you have when you observe something. We need to remember that events can stimulate feelings within us, but people do not cause us to feel a certain way. Once we own our feelings, we have the choice of changing them. If we believe others cause our feelings, we have no control or possibility of changing our feelings and are helpless. Allowing ourselves to be vulnerable by expressing our feelings can help resolve disagreements.

4. State a need not being met. Our feelings are indicators of needs we have. We first have to understand what needs we have and then we can get those needs met. Dr. William Glasser identified 5 basic needs we all share: love and belonging (respected, sharing, cooperation), power (recognition, success, importance), fun (enjoyment, learning, change), survival (health, food, warmth) , and freedom (choices, independence, opportunities). What is it that you need and what would you like to request of the other person in relation to those needs?

5. Make a specific request based on needs. A request is a respectful way of asking for something to be done differently. A request is different than a demand.

6. End with another positive statement. Appreciate what is going well and share your gratitude.

SCENARIO:

Fourth grader is dismissed twenty minutes early every afternoon. His parents are concerned about what he is missing every day and that he is on a special education bus. The school staff has told the parents there is nothing they can do because it is based on the bus schedule.

Example:

Father's response using compassionate communication:

"My wife and I are happy Pablo is included in his fourth grade class and showing so much growth. We have seen how he is dropped off at home every day at 3:30. We know school is dismissed at 3:30. Pablo told us he gets on the special education bus at 3:10. We are worried about what he is missing at the end of the day and also are concerned he is not riding the regular school bus, even though he is included all day in his fourth grade class. We believe his sense of being a full member of his fourth grade class is jeopardized when he leaves his classroom everyday 20 minutes before anyone else and has to ride the special education bus. We are requesting a meeting to amend his IEP so he can be dismissed at 3:30 and ride the typical school bus. Thank you for providing the support for Pablo to be successful in fourth grade."

ANALYSIS:

Notice how the father in the example above followed all of the 6 steps of compassionate communication. You can use this strategy for both verbal and written communication.

DID YOU KNOW:

When you have an important question to think about and formulate an answer to, your brain sends blood to the parts of your brain to help you think, and away from the parts of your body that send you into fight, flight, or freeze mode. Pretty interesting, huh? So, when you feel like you are being confronted with harsh, angry comments, ask yourself some questions and get the blood flowing to help you think instead of going into the fight, flight, or freeze mode. Here are examples of what you could ask yourself:

* What does my child really need?

* What do I really need from others?

* What do I really want my relationship with this person to be like?

* How could I behave if I really wanted these results?

How to Respond to Negative Behavior

It is common for people to respond to inappropriate behavior with more inappropriate behavior. Of course, this is not effective. What else could parents do when confronted with negative behavior? Look at the next page for some ideas.

How to Respond to Negative Behavior

Behavior of Other Person	Your Response
Insist on their solution.	Don't argue. Assume they have a valid reason for their position. Ask questions to understand their underlying interests.
Attack your position.	Use this as a chance to clarify your interests. Be open to criticism and advice from school staff. Then explain your interests and why they are important.
Attack you personally.	Ask questions and repeat their responses back to them to make sure you understood what they said.
Make unreasonable demands.	Ask questions, then pause. If there is silence, don't say anything. Many times the other party will begin talking to fill the silence.
Purposeful deception.	Address the tactic being used, but don't do it in an insulting way. Discuss the tactic in order to make it less effective.
Using their power over you.	Remember you have power as a parent, as one who intimately knows your child.
Don't take you seriously.	Be open about your feelings. This will build credibility.
School staff are always arguing.	Tell a story instead of arguing.
Staff won't listen to you.	Begin by acknowledging they have the power to accept or reject your ideas.

It is important to let go of unproductive behavior the "Old You" used so the "New You" shines through at meetings.

The Old You

When You Do This	These Are The Likely Results
You sit back quietly even though you disagree.	Rarely committed to the final decision. Ideas remain in your head, your opinions are never shared End up quietly criticizing and passively resisting.
Believing that others are the cause of all the problems.	Put yourself in the victim's role.
Verbal attacks, discredit others	Harm others Start looking for ways to win and punish others.

The New You

When You Change & Do This	These Are The New Results
You respectfully share your ideas and opinions.	Healthy discussions happen, one idea leads to another, a quality decision is reached. You support the final decision
Believe the best way to work on "us" is to start with "me".	Conversation stays focused on what the student needs Encourage the flow of conversation even when there are different opinions and strong emotions.
Use Compassionate Communication	Everyone benefits. Catch problems before they become major disagreements.

CALL TO ACTION:

Download these 3 handouts and review them before IEP meetings or parent-teacher conferences:

Compassionate Communication - the 6 steps for sharing your thoughts, feelings, a need you have, and to make a request.

http://bit.ly/1j8Ca2o

How to Respond to Negative Behaviors – a handy chart to remind yourself of effective ways to respond to behaviors that are stopping the collaboration process. http://bit.ly/1LnenT0

The Old You and The New You - a great reminder of unproductive behavior to avoid and what you can do instead. Download it here

http://bit.ly/1kG3RkF

RESOURCES:

How To Compromise With Your School District Without Compromising *Your Child* by Gary Mayerson

This is a helpful website, The Center for Non Violence Communication: http://www.cnvc.org/

Critical Conversations: Tools For Talking When Stakes Are High by Kerry Patterson, Ron McMillan, and Al Swizzler

Always remember you are braver than you believe,

stronger than you seem, and smarter than you think.

Christopher Robin

Chapter 5: Building Authentic Relationships

People fail to get along because they fear each other;

they fear each other because they don't know

each other;

they don't know each other because

they have not communicated with each other.

Martin Luther King Jr.

I tell parents the three Rs of Advocacy are: Relationships, Relationships, and Relationships. One way of building relationships is to share success stories - dwell in the positive for awhile. Both educators and parents can share examples of what has worked with the child. This can help promote collaboration and generate new ideas and strategies to try. Be open to doing things a new way.

You want the school year to be one when your child is happier, safer, and learning more than ever, so get ready to partner with his teachers and support people. A successful education for students requires a healthy partnership between parents and educators. When there is regular two-way communication and an agreement to work together, your child wins.

Another element in building relationships is having a trusting foundation. You know trust is built over time, based on on-going interactions, and with consistent behavior by both sides. If parents and school staff do not interact on a regular basis, positive relationships will take longer to develop.

I bet you want other children to recognize qualities they have in common with your child, so they can appreciate each other and build friendships. Well guess what? You need to commit to finding qualities, philosophies, interests, and values that you share with school staff. Even if you just strike up a conversation and discover you are both from the same home state, or you both have the same favorite restaurant in town, those can be the seeds to growing a relationship. It can be challenging for people in conflict to identify what beliefs or points of view that they have in common with others. The most important shared interest should be doing what is needed for the child.

Stay in close touch with your child's teacher, via email, written notes, phone calls, and/or in-person meetings. Agree on the frequency of these communications, and honor that commitment. Frequent communication prevents months going by without realizing there are successes to celebrate or concerns to address.

It is important for parents to develop positive relationships with the people who touch their children's lives days in and out. Just as we want educators to recognize and value our children's strengths and interests, we need to show our appreciation for their strengths and the positive impact they have on our children's lives.

WHY:

Developing a quality relationship between parents and educators will lead to positive outcomes for students. That is what we are all about - the child.

There are many positive effects of collaborative relationships between parents and educators. These include: higher achievement for students, more engaged families, stronger support for schools and improved teacher morale and teacher performance.

WHAT PARENTS CAN DO:

1. Build trust by sharing your vision of your child's life as an adult. See the #1 Bonus at the end of this chapter for tips on creating vision statements. The purpose of the vision statement is to open your eyes to what is possible. Visions written down are more likely to be achieved. Visions kept in your mind just remain as wishes. The keys to having a clear and compelling vision are to use a variety of ways to show and embrace your vision. Your vision can be shared through pictures and words. You want it to be appealing to the mind and emotions.

2. Describe your child as a real person, a whole person. Do not define your child by his label. Let others first become connected to your child as a person.

3. Put aside your assumptions about others and instead, spend time learning about them, from them. Turn a stranger into a person you know. Get to know staff as people: learn their likes and dislikes, discover commonalities, etc. People will go the extra mile for those they're connected to.

4. Respect the other person's "Model of the World". Respect the rights of others to have different values and beliefs. Value the differences and learn from them.

5. Turn your Receive button on and turn your Transmit button off (listen more than you talk).

6. Give permission for mistakes to be made. Teachers often feel worried they are going to disappoint parents (especially if you have a reputation for being one of "those parents") if things do not go exactly right. As parents, we have all made mistakes and learned along the way. I bet you

can think of some mistakes you have made, share those with teachers. Let them know you do not expect perfection from others.

7. Focus on positives and demonstrate gratitude. Everyone appreciates being recognized when things are going well. You know what a difference it makes if you get a phone call from the school to share some good news. Well, guess what? Teachers and administrators also appreciate hearing some positive feedback. Doing this one thing goes a long way in building healthy relationships.

8. Send birthday greetings, recognize support staff on administrative assistant day, thank lunchroom helpers, bring baked goodies to nursing staff, etc. A little effort can generate big smiles! In this day and age of technology, do not forget about a handwritten note of thanks. It does not have to be long, but a written note every once in a while will surprise and delight the person receiving it.

9. Recognize there will be times when extra effort is needed to develop relationships. Relationships between families and people paid to be in children's lives are similar to arranged marriages. We might not have chosen this person to work with, but with open communication, we can see positive results.

10. Listen to yourself, first. Before sending a letter, read it out loud first, and/or practice what you're going to say in the mirror. Listen to the thoughts you have and the feelings in your gut. What is it you want others to understand? Does that come across in your letter, or do you need to revise it? Chapter 4: Know What To Say When, will give you more examples of how to phrase things.

11. Nurture relationships. Everyone involved must work to sustain the partnerships. If you feel like a teacher or administrator is not responding to your attempts to build a relationship, think about asking another parent who knows the people involved if they have any tips for you, or things that have worked for them.

12. Use pronouns such as, we, and our instead of I, and mine. The little change in language can make a big difference. It is about a team of people, the whole village working together for your child.

13. Identify points of agreement. When having a conversation, start with what you agree with, or ask questions you know the other person will answer with a "Yes." Build on these areas of common ground.

14. Keep everyone on the same page. Pass on relevant articles, websites, and ideas to teachers. Tell them you are interested in any resources they can share with you. Have this be a back-and-forth relationship.

As you plan your communication with teachers and other staff members, remember it is understandable that these conversations can become very emotional. You care deeply for your child and want him to be safe, successful, and happy at school. Become aware of when you feel your emotions are beginning to overcome the message you want understood. Just like we want our children to be aware of when they are becoming stressed, recognize their triggers, and have a positive way to deal with it - parents also need to know how to do this. Here are some steps that can be taken:

1. Visualize what your ideal working relationship with teachers would look like, feel like. Then decide what your behaviors and interactions will need to look like in order to create that ideal working relationship. Perhaps, in the past you have had positive relationships with a teacher. What did that look like, feel like? How did you interact with that teacher? How can you replicate that with your child's current school team? Define and share what you want, be willing to listen to and meet others' desires. Work to create relationships that you're both proud of.

2. Plan and even rehearse what you are going to say. Here is where taking the time to practice with someone else will help you feel more confident. The more confident you are, the less emotional the discussion will be.

3. Remember, you get what you anticipate. If you are worried about your child's next IEP meeting and are expecting a battle, that is what you'll get.

We've probably heard of the self-fulfilling prophecy - it is an assumption that causes people to behave in certain ways and the end result is their assumption becomes a reality. Instead, decide what you want the IEP meeting to be like, visualize it going well, anticipate it being a positive meeting!

4. We want teachers to expect the best from our children and know they will rise to the high expectations. We need to model that same behavior when we are working with school staff members. Expect the IEP team members to be positive and focused on your child's growth and chances are, the meeting will go more smoothly.

The Inclusive Class Podcast

I was interviewed for The Inclusive Class's podcast on how to have less drama at IEP meetings. Below is a transcript of the podcast. If you would rather listen to the podcast, see Bonus #2 at the end of this chapter for the audio link.

Transcription

TERRI:

Good morning and welcome to The Inclusive Class podcast, through interviews and discussions it's our goal to explore the promise and practice of inclusive education.

NICOLE:

I am Nicole Eredicts one of your host for the show, The Inclusive Class. This morning is my co-host Terry Mauro. Good morning, Terri.

TERRI:

Good morning, Nicole and welcome to all our listeners. I am Terry Mauro, I am the author of 50 Ways to Support Your Child's Special Education and I write about special needs for about.com at specialchildren.about.com And I would like to mention to anybody out there listening to us live that we are not taking phone calls but the chat room will be open if you'd like to stop in and suggest a question. I'll try to work it in if we have time, then again because this is the first week of Lent and I have given up coffee until Easter I may be asleep by the time you type your message in and I will never see it. So if I am unduly sluggish or snappish during this next half hour you will understand that I am in caffeine withdrawal.

NICOLE:

This is our third round with, you know, that we are doing the caffeine withdrawal shows.

TERRI:

Yep, yep every year. I've been doing it for quite some time so this is the third year with the podcast and I've been doing it in my life before that. Yeah it's a good thing to give up. But the first few days are headachy and crappy. Which my husband says is evidence that I should give it up for good and never get it back. That's probably not going to happen.

NICOLE:

See what it does to you!

TERRI:

Anyway trying to make it through the week and then eventually I'll be fine.

NICOLE:

Good. Well at least you don't have an IEP meeting to go to today.

TERRI:

That is true! I would possibly snap off some heads.

NICOLE:

We were talking about that earlier.

TERRI:

Yes, yes, very happy never to have another IEP meeting in my future. I don't know maybe for a grandchild. I may have to go and bop some heads together, but not for a long time.

NICOLE:

You're done with it?

TERRI:

Well I know I am happy to be done with it and I am hearing all the blog post and the Facebook posts trying to come through now from people who are going to IEP meetings.

NICOLE:

Yeah it's that time of year.

TERRI:

So I can tell all of them and you know, I just want to give all of them a big hug. From the parents perspective it's difficult and I know from the professional end it's probably difficult also for different reasons. But you know if we're talking about dealing with less drama that would be good to know how one does that.

NICOLE:

Well...

TERRI:

It seem like there is always drama of some sort.

NICOLE:

Yeah it's something unexpected or.....

TERRI:

Best of preparation and planning, smoozing and bringing cookies to the child's IEP to take them all through the years and there is still drama at the child's IEP meetings.

NICOLE:

But you all know its stressful time, that's for sure.

TERRI:

It certainly is, yeah one that I am glad to be rid of although I missed the opportunity to talk to...college professors don't want to talk to you.

TERRI:

They just probably didn't want to talk to me either but they had to. College professors don't have to.

NICOLE:

You've had your fair share that's for sure.

TERRI:

I have indeed.

NICOLE:

For many years as well being the parent on the other side of that table. Of course being the teacher in that room as well.

TERRI:

You've seen both sides as well.

NICOLE:

Yeah, definitely interesting. I definitely know the emotions, and the levels of concern or frustration or excitement that a parent can have and then I know from a teacher that the limitations that we're restrained by as a school, as to what we can provide and what we can offer and what realistically can happen. Yeah it's definitely an interesting experience. That's when the emotions run high.

TERRI:

I think intellectually parents understand I mean they're tax payers too and understand what the limitations are and how with the school you're going to understand intellectually that the way its often presented is a less than straight forward way. Kind of adds to the injury of it and still then, it's your kid. You're sympathetic, you can't afford this but that's what your kid needs, you gotta fight for it. I mean you can't just say 'that's ok, never mind. just put my kid back in the classroom and don't teach him anything. So it's a battle, it really is. And even when everybody understands and everybody has the best of intentions they're still just institutional differences that can't be avoided. But hopefully we'll be able to find some ways to deal with that stuff in a more civilized and grown up manner.

NICOLE:

Yeah well we have definitely. Our guest today is definitely experienced at not only the IEP level in terms of being a parent but also as a teacher. And I'm sure she'll have lots of advice and tips for us today because I think above all we all want what's best for our kids. Whether they're our own child or our student.

TERRI:

Yea, one would like to think that.

NICOLE:

And you wouldn't want to go in there battling and feeling like we're really struggling to get somewhere. We want it to be successful. So I'm going to introduce our expert guest and find out what she has to say because yeah we all have our personal experiences with it but I'm excited to see how other people deal with it as well. So what better way to find out than to talk to Charmaine Thaner who is an advocate for parents and has over 30 years of teaching as well to add to her diverse background and her unique perspectives she brings to families and helping them advocate for their child at school and helping them get what they need during IEP meetings. And she has some also, like I said she's got lots of years in the classroom, as a special educator, a parent and a teacher and a university professor or instructor and she continues to support parents now as an advocate and public speaker through her work and business called Collaborative Special Education Advocacy. So I'm going to introduce her this morning and we'll get started with our questions. Good Morning Charmaine how are you?

CHARMAINE:

Good morning, I am great!

NICOLE:

Good, good thank you for joining us this morning and always excited to, I know you've always been interactive on social media quite a bit so it's always exciting to talk with somebody who you usually normally chat with or make a comment to online so it's kind of neat that we get to do this so thank you for joining us this morning.

I just want to start by asking you why after 30 years of teaching you decide to become a parent advocate because you just took one hat off and put another one on. So what's the reason for your transition?

CHARMAINE:

Well you know I did it because I've been there, done that and I have the T-shirt to show it. I know what it's like to be a parent sitting at that big conference table and feeling overwhelmed and frustrated and as Terri said, it's real emotional when you talking about your child. And I felt like what I could do next is to help parents and kind of be that guide on the side so they can make sure their kids gets the education they deserve.

NICOLE:

Yeah, I mean definitely I think from the teacher point of view we can offer a few more tips and advice you know that we might not be able to say out loud in an actual meeting.

CHARMAINE:

Right.

TERRI:

And it's a feeling that there are things that good people can't say out a loud in a meeting that often time turns a parents off. You know that, you know that there is some stuff that you don't know about. And you find it frustrating.

NICOLE:

And that's the thing teachers don't go into IEP meetings wanting to create a difficult situation [00:08:56.09] and as I mentioned we all want what's best for the kids in their class. And of course parents don't want to go in with a lot of drama and anxiety. But how can a parent approach an IEP meeting without those high emotions and anxiety and feelings of dread?

CHARMAINE:

Well I think you know you both talked about that a little bit at the start of the podcast. I think preparation is going to make a difference, but I think we're still going to feel those emotions as parents. One of the things I always try to do is to stay focused on that big picture and vision for Dylan that we had. So when you are in the IEP meeting one of the things that you can do is to look at the decisions that we are going to make right now. Is it going to help us move forward to that big picture, to that vision that we have for our child? Stay focused on that vs. sometimes an adult issue that gets in our way and causes the drama. So if we can focus on our child and know that this IEP is going to take us one step closer to where we want to our child to be at after they have graduated from high school, I think that helps a lot.

NICOLE:

Now, do you recommend, this sort of leads me into my next question, but do you recommend parents to speak to the teacher before an IEP meeting or just go to the IEP meeting?

CHARMAINE:

I think that's a great idea to go ahead and meet ahead of the time. Some people are like what I have to schedule another meeting?! But I think because in the IEP meeting the time is really condensed and it's hard to get as much discussions going that I think to write an effective IEP. So by meeting ahead I think you can ask some questions to try to get a better understanding of where your child is, you know, performing right now in the classroom and any concerns that the teachers have. And you can talk about your perspective of what you've seen the child bring home as far as class work. Try to get an understanding because that first part of the IEP meeting is when you talk about strengths and needs and present levels. These are the foundations of the IEP. So if you could have some of that preliminary understanding but you still want to, when you have the actual IEP meeting, you still want to capture that discussion and those main points to make sure that it's written in the IEP.

NICOLE:

It's great to have some sort of discussion beforehand and that's some good tips, good ways to ask without coming across as being defensive, or overly assertive or aggressive. It's also a way of getting more information and also making the point that, can you be more specific, I want to know how this is going to look because this is important. Exactly, maybe develop a new understanding of the situation as well. Because sometimes a teacher doesn't have time or the support staff doesn't have time to fully explore and explain what the child is presenting or doing at school. It'd be nice to have that time for background information.

Is there any communication tip you can give to teachers as well as parents in terms of approaching the IEP meeting and interacting with other people?

CHARMAINE:

Sure, I think for teachers, what I tried to do was to make a list of all the things the student could do. So, when I went to the IEP meeting I could go through that list. I could also hand a copy to the family. Because, I think when we start out IEP meetings with talking about deficits and weaknesses parents just, you can just physically see them shutting down. So, a tip for teachers is to make a list of things the student can do, their strengths, their interests that you've noticed in class, what they actually can do and make sure you give parents a copy of that so they have something to take home and go, "Wow these are positive things about my child."

The tip that would go both for parents and educators would be to do in the IEP meeting, is to ask more questions. I think of how many times when we hear somebody saying something, kind of our initial thing is, "Well wait until I can respond and I can't wait until they stop talking so I can get my point across." And we lose that ability to really hear what they're saying. So, asking clarifying questions or probing questions, I mean that is a typical kind of communication skill, but that's really, really helpful during an IEP meeting, so we don't make assumptions. We can be walking in there with this whole scenario playing in our head about how they're not going to do this for our kid, or how they don't do this, and that scenario playing in our head can really cause more drama. So, if we can take a step back, ask questions like, "What would it take to do..." whatever the issue is. Or, "Can you give me some examples of what you're describing?" Or, "What I heard you say was..." and repeat it back. Because some times when we're not getting their point of view and we do not understand their message - that is really crucial.

TERRI:

Those are good tips. I know a lot of parents now once they get a little experience under their belt sometimes they go into IEP meetings in a very confrontational way. I've spoken to groups of parents where some of them just think they have the scalps of IEP members hanging from their, you know, rear view mirror. Like they're so proud of the time they got this person into trouble, or they got this person...... or they read this person the riot act at an IEP meeting. And as much a parents often feel attacked in IEP meetings, sometimes I think we can be too eager to make it a war, when really it should be a meeting of equals where all of us with experience sit down and talk like adults.

CHARMAINE:

I think that's where we get back to keeping that focus on your child. The other thing that I think really helps a lot is to actually have your child attend a meeting with you. I mean that makes a huge difference to the tone of the meeting. Dylan always went to his meetings even when he was real young. We started by having meetings at our house and when he was like two years old, so he could be there playing with his toys, you know, his dog and everything, but people could see him, a neat typical kid versus reading his records and making impressions. It made us feel more comfortable. Then when he was in Kindergarten we would have our IEP meetings, well we had our IEP meetings in his Kindergarten class. He was there he could play at the different centers but because Dylan was present, I think that helped to change the tone of the meeting. And people are a little more conscious of, it really is about the kid, and if we've got adult, issues we'll deal with that later.

TERRI:

Yeah, that's definitely, neither of my kids ever wanted to go to IEP meetings, even when they were in High School, they were sort of like "Do I have to?" But yes, certainly there's a value in keeping the focus that way. You know some parents also bring pictures, put pictures of their kid on the top of the bunch of records they are bringing and then have that prominently displayed on the table, this is reality we are talking about, not some abstract. But it's interesting when you talk about emotions in IEP meetings, the most emotional IEP meeting I ever had was one where everybody was of goodwill and everybody was focused on what was right for the child but there was a fundamental difference of opinion as to what that was. And so I felt very strongly one way and the Child Study team people, who loved my daughter felt that what I was suggesting would be horrible for her. They felt that they were defending her, and it was just the most awful thing, Really, really hurtful things were said about her potential and about what I had to realize, and I'm sure they felt the things that I was saying were demeaning to them, that they weren't doing their jobs, and, what do you do when you're in a situation like that when emotions are running so high?

There are all different scenarios in which emotions can take over in a meeting that was certainly one of them. You know, and from both the parent and from the professional side, what can be done when emotions get that high? Other than, like everybody saying "Let's pick this up later."

CHARMAINE:

Right, right, I know and I guess, well that teacher part of me I come with looking at the three Rs of what to do when emotions are running that high. It's to Relax, Regroup and then to Respond. So the relaxing is noticing different things in your body, like are your knees starting to go up and down under the table, are you starting to breathe faster, are you like pinching yourself. So when you start seeing or feeling those physical kinds of things beforehand, take a few deep breaths, you know, and just try to exhale that tension, so that's like a physical kind of thing. But then, to regroup and to think for just for a couple of seconds and to remind yourself that we're talking about your child here and we want to keep that big picture in mind. And then the other part for responding that I have done and I have helped parents use, is the, it's kind of like a simple process of, first you say what you have noticed or what you've observed and you do that in a non-judgmental way. Then you say what you are feeling, the third thing is what you need and then the fourth thing is that you should make a specific request.

So an example, would be what you've observed. You could say, "I've noticed when we're talking about the least restrictive environment for Jason I begin feeling frustrated because I really have a need for Jason to have that sense of belonging in the classroom. So I'm requesting we take a break for a few minutes and then when we come back let's hear from Jason and his perspective." So, those steps help I think center us and get us and away from reacting with emotions so you say what you've observed, what you're feeling, what your need is and then make a request.

The other thing that I think in the example that you gave us is, and it gets into a little bit more as far as negotiating kind of thing, but it's the difference between somebody's position and their interest. Often times when we are arguing and we are getting into that relentless debate we are not getting to the underlying issue of why we are taking that position and why we are planting the 'flag' right there.

TERRI:

Yeah, yeah, that's a good point.

NICOLE:

Hmm, I like those...the four points to the three: relax, regroup and respond, a nice way of remembering how to approach that.

TERRI:

Often times I don't know how it is in other districts but in our districts IEPs are just scheduled to every inch of their lives and everybody else have some place they need to be so the real feeling is that we have to get through this and we have to make a decision before you know. I can't imagine in most all of the IEP meetings I have been in saying we take a break and come back because you'll lose half the room. But certainly that would be a lot of the time, what needs to happen is let's get out all the frustrations and then we meet again to talk about them. You know to offload and calm down.

CHARMAINE:

And it could, right.

TERRI:

But administratively...Exactly.

CHARMAINE:

And it's not like, yeah, and I totally understand because most of them are like an hour and we've got somebody else waiting in the hall for the next one. So, it's not like we can take a 10 minute break, maybe you, let's take a break from our conversation and let's hear this or let's do this or you know so you just make kind of like a break between now we've been kind of going back and forth and we are kind of stuck. Let's take a break put that on the parking lot or whatever and move on. Sometimes that will help.

TERRI:

Yeah, that's a good idea and when you're talking about having a meeting with the teacher beforehand I've always felt that to be really useful because at least you have somebody who is on the same page as you or at least you know what page they are on before you walk into that room but also if you can; I don't know if you did this but if you can be a presence in the school throughout the year and in the classroom.

I used to work in the library so teachers always had access to me and I always had access to them and I could see what was going on, I could watch my kids classes and see what the dynamics were between the teachers and the aides and the different kids and each other and there would always be an informal way to say things that you don't want to have to say formally in that room but you can say you know, "Hey, I see this isn't working could you try that or something like that?" And then you are more of a known quantity when you sit in the room. You are not somebody they see once a year and you know, argue with and you can have a lot of these discussions informally in a less emotional context.

CHARMAINE:

Yeah that's a great idea and I think that's where it comes down to. Like I tell families that, you know, the three RS of advocacy are relationship, relationships and relationships. So as much as we can do that you know, be like you said, be a known quantity in the building and be able to have those informal discussions throughout the year, because it shouldn't just be one hour meeting.

TERRI:

Yeah, definitely, and you can even sometimes chat up the child's study team members if you know where their offices is, pass by and if there is no meeting going on, just poke your head in and say "By the way Johnny is doing great or he is you know..., we need to keep our eye on this." Or something like that so it's not all saved up for one hour in the Spring.

NICOLE:

I have a quick question, sorry I just came up with it and I just want to throw it in there. I know as a teacher then as a parent too, I have spoken with quite a few parents who are wanting to advocate for their child going into an IEP meeting, and there is a lot of emotions going on in there. We've talked a lot about anger and hostility and I find that a lot of that stems from, and I can tell because they are referring back to their own school experiences, and their own concepts of what school is about. Is there any advice you could give to parents in terms of what their perspective should be in going in or what their attitude should be? Do you have anything specific?

CHARMAINE:

Yeah, and I think that's true and I think you see it not only in our IEP meetings but when it comes to time for parents teachers conferences and families that don't have positive school experiences aren't going to be the ones to sign up to come to the parents conferences. So as teachers we need to be cognizant of that and have multiple ways of parents providing their input. When you look at the formal meetings like the IEP, I think there are tips that we talked about as far as try to talk ahead of time and if families don't feel comfortable in school to talk to parents, saying what's the best way to do that. Say let's make a phone call or is there a way we can touch base through email. I think they need to desensitize that and help the parents moved through that and know that this is going to be a new day, a new situation and that things are different now. Hanging onto those past experiences, like parents who have had a negative IEP meeting in the past and then coming into the next one, you know you've got to release that because that's not going to be helpful for your kid.

NICOLE:

Definitely, yeah sorry Terri thanks you for allowing me to interject there.

TERRI:

That's ok that's a good observation. Yeah that's a good question, certainly parent teacher conference are something that, you know if you talking about relationships and with having a dialogue throughout the year. I can't understand why anybody passes those up, I would have them more often if I could. I would always go to those, and you can often find out a bunch of some of the issues that are going on through that. It's often times the people who most need to go to those who don't and I know that's often frustrating for teachers and then they go into the meetings with that frustration and it just makes everything worse.

Yeah, certainly for people to do that, it's important. And an important way of preparing and avoiding the drama. But I know that back to school nights fewer and fewer parents are coming to them, but I would go to them. Sometimes I would get a one on one meeting with the teacher if none of the parents came, so that's a good piece of advice to get out there for people.

Unfortunately, it's the end of our time and I want to thank you for being our guest today. It's a great topic to talk about and good information to get out to people. And I would like to thank our listeners for tuning into our program this morning. We will be back next week at the same time with our guest Jennifer Curtis about modifying and adapting class work for students.

In the meantime you can follow us on Facebook and Twitter where Nicole tweets under the name inclusiveclass class I am at mamatude. And finally you can download our past podcasts for free on Sticher or iTunes. Just want to make a mention here since we have a couple of seconds, that if people who are interested in watching the Winter Para-Olympics they start today and in fact coverage starts today on NBCSN which you may have somewhere on your cable network, at 11:00am. You can start watching the opening ceremony or start DVRing them as I am and there will be some more coverage on NBC and NBCSN and also available online. You should be able to find that information. It's a really good opportunity to watch with your child to see what people with disability can do, cause it's awesome.

Bye everybody and have a great week. Goodbye. Thank you.

End of Transcription

CALL TO ACTION:

Tell at least one friend about what you have been learning from this book. When you teach others the new skills you have learned, it helps you use these newfound ideas with more confidence.

RESOURCES:

This is one of my favorite sites for family-school partnerships. They offer webinars, publications, and other resources. Harvard Family Research Project: www.hfrp.org

A recommended article about building parent - school relationships

http://bit.ly/1MprYwY

The National PTA (Parent Teacher Association) has six standards for Family - School Partnerships. How would your school rate?

http://bit.ly/1FxqMF5

BONUSES:

#1 Bonus: Parent/student vision statement

The parent/student vision statement is critical to share at each IEP meeting. Yes, I said, at each IEP meeting. It is important to set the tone of the meeting with the big picture of what success will look like for your child. As your child gets older, it becomes their vision statement, what they want their life to look like.

There are an endless variety of ways to develop your vision statement. Some families have cut out pictures from magazines, or used clip art from the internet or let photos describe their vision. Some students prefer to make a PowerPoint to share about the life they want to achieve. Other examples of vision statements: a simple video can be made with a computer or cell phone, copies of a written statement can be shared with the team members, or a story can be told. The key is to have a clear and compelling vision, one that appeals to the mind and emotions.

Remember that the purpose of the vision statement is to inspire, energize, motivate, and stimulate creativity, not to be a way to measure success; that is the job of the IEP goals and objectives. What do you want your child's life to look like when they're adults? Where and how will they live and work? What about relationships? How will they pursue their passions and interests?

Tips for developing a vision statement:

• Describe your vision statement in present tense as if you are reporting what you actually see, hear, think and feel after your ideal outcome is realized.

• Make your vision statement emotional. Your vision statement should describe how you will feel when the outcome is realized. Including an emotional payoff in your vision statement will make it even more compelling, inspiring, and energizing.

• Add sensory details. The more sensory details you can provide, the more powerful your statement becomes. Describe the scenes, colors, sounds, and shapes. Describe who is there and what everyone is doing. These sensory details will help you build a more complete and powerful mental image of your ideal outcome.

#2 Bonus:

If you're more of an auditory learner, listen to the podcast, IEP Meetings With Less Drama, when I was interviewed for The Inclusive Class

www.theinclusiveclass.com/2014/03/iep-meetings-with-less-drama.html

> Become a possibilitarian.
>
> No matter how dark things seem to be
>
> or actually are,
>
> raise your sights and see possibilities —
>
> always see them, for they're always there.
>
> — Norman Vincent Peale

Chapter 6: How To Use Collaborative Problem Solving

The secret of change is to focus all of your energy, not on fighting the old, but on building the new.

Socrates

Ever attended a meeting at school and felt like:

• the staff had already made up their mind about things before even coming to the meeting? Let's be honest, how many of us parents also have our minds made up before we go to the meeting?

• the arguing and debating just goes on and on?

• the teachers and administrators keep saying, "But this is how we do it."?

• people feel so defensive and angry that there is no way issues are going to be resolved?

The good news is, meetings do not have to be like that. An important step for collaborative problem solving is being open to gathering new insights and envisioning new possibilities!

Also, if you can view the conflict as a specific set of circumstances and not because of the person you are talking to, you are more apt to resolve the conflict and still be able to have working relationships with the people involved.

WHY:

Your child will have the chance to shine when given the right opportunities. When you explore options and think outside of the special education box, a new world of possibilities exists. Here are some ideas to get you started with possibility thinking for the education world.

WHAT PARENTS CAN DO:

1. Challenge:

Families, students, and educators can challenge widely held assumptions about the potential of students with disability labels. To create new possibilities for students, it will often involve questioning what has always been done. Everyone can set a challenge for themselves to use a student's strengths/preferences/interests to teach new skills and introduce new concepts.

2. Connect:

Often when a student's significant support needs are described, an immediate association is made that the student will need to be placed in a separate special education classroom. When these common associations are made continually, it decreases the ability to see new possibilities. Practice making new connections between seemingly unrelated questions, problems, or ideas to jumpstart creative thinking.

3. Visualize:

The thoughts and beliefs of adults and students can limit or expand the number of opportunities available. Create a poster(s) of images and quotations that are inspirational and represent goals to accomplish. Share the posters at the next IEP meeting to encourage creative thinking. Visualize each part of the IEP meeting going well, imagine a positive outcome, and the mental barriers that have been roadblocks in the past will be lessened.

4. Collaborate:

Honoring all team members' input will allow the visions to be realized. Dissolve turf boundaries and service provider (Occupational Therapist, Speech/Language Pathologist, Physical Therapist) specific goals. Instead write goals for the student that all team members can support and help the student achieve. Encourage interaction between groups that do not often attend IEP meetings. Chances are the specialty (Art, P.E., Music) and elective teachers have terrific ideas that could be tried.

5. Motivate:

Think of new ideas that have an emotional appeal. Ask what is worth doing and what can the student get excited about. Have the student write down his goals and dreams and how they make him feel. The feelings attached to his goals will be his greatest source of motivation.

6. Improvise:

When a technique is not working, improvise, and try something new. Give permission for everyone to experiment. Make daily deposits in idea banks and when needed, pick a new idea to try.

7. Reorient:

Change your assumptions into, "How can we?" Reframe problems and then different solutions will emerge. Facilitate a discussion with the student and peers. Get their input and perspectives. Chances are, you'll get some practical ideas that adults would never have come up with.

SCENARIO:

Special Education Director:

Well, we have come to that time in the meeting where we need to decide the placement for the student.

Parent:

Yes, I understand we will be discussing options so he can be in the least restrictive environment.

Special Education Director:

Yes, we need to look at the programs we have that will meet his needs.

Parent:

Are you saying that we will only look at existing ways to provide my son the supports and services he needs?

Special Education Director:

Well, the district does offer a wonderful special education preschool class that is taught by an awesome special education early childhood teacher and there are two very experienced paraprofessionals that also work in the classroom.

Parent:

I have heard good feedback about the special education preschool. I am wondering if we could spend a few minutes brainstorming where else Trevor could get his needs met.

Special Education Director:

I am not sure that would be time well spent. We already know the district special ed preschool class is a great fit for the little ones that are showing developmental delays.

Parent:

I do think we want to discuss the district preschool class as an option and other possibilities. When we look back to what we have written in Trevor's IEP so far, there are many needs that revolve around him being with some typical, same-aged peers in order to have opportunities for increasing his play skills, and conversation skills. Trevor has also shown us he is really motivated to try harder when he is with typical peers.

Special Education Early Childhood Teacher:

I'm just not sure there are any other options for Trevor. What were you thinking of?

Parent:

Well, let's think of where other preschoolers spend their day. Some are at home with a stay-at-home parent or babysitter, others go to a day care center or day care home, some are at church's preschools, and there are community preschools in centers. Can we think of other places where preschoolers spend their day?

Special Education Early Childhood Teacher:

Those are places for typical kids to go to, they are not options for kids like Trevor with developmental delays.

Advocate:

I think Mrs. Anderson is asking the team to consider the district preschool class and less restrictive environments.

Special Education Director:

How in the world do you expect a little guy to get the special help he needs if he is being babysat all day at his house?

Parent:

You are right, we need to make sure Trevor can get the services and supports he needs if he was served outside of the district special education classroom. Since Trevor's needs are mainly language based, one option could be Trevor goes to a community preschool and the speech/language therapist would go to that community preschool twice a week and work with him there during activities with his friends.

Special Education Director:

We don't have extra speech therapists that can be driving around town to go to a community preschool when we have a special ed preschool class right in our elementary building.

Parent:

We believe Trevor's needs can be most appropriately met in a less restrictive classroom.

Special Education Director:

How would a community preschool teacher get enough help to know what to do with Trevor when the speech therapist isn't there?

Parent:

That is a good point! I know in the schools sometimes the therapist will also have some time she can consult with the teacher besides the time she works with the child.

Special Education Early Childhood Teacher:

Therapists usually consult with elementary teachers, but I guess they could also have some consultation time with a community preschool teacher.

Special Education Director:

I am not sure how any of this would work, but I am willing to explore it and get back with the IEP team next week.

Parent:

Thank you! I appreciate your willingness to look at other options.

ANALYSIS:

The parent helped the staff challenge the thinking that the only option was a special education preschool class. The team also considered how a student's needs can be met when a speech/language therapist provides direct services at a community preschool and collaborates with the preschool teacher.

Positions and Interests:

Discovering what is Really Important

A crucial step to resolve conflicts is to be able to tell the difference between positions and interests. If parents or school staff "dig in their heels" based on a position they have, there will be little resolution. When both sides become personally committed to their positions, often egos can become intertwined with issues, and people will do what they have to do in order to save face.

Instead, when both parties talk about the underlying needs (interests) they have, it can help identify common ground and result in more positive agreements.

WHY:

Once you get passed your and the other person's position (that one solution wanted) and instead identify your and the other person's interests (underlying values and needs people want met), it is much easier to resolve differences. This will allow true collaboration to happen, relationships can be built and hostility reduced.

WHAT PARENTS CAN DO:

1. Watch this short video from CADRE: The National Center on Dispute Resolution in Special Education to get a better sense of how positions and interests are different. Yes, stop reading the book for a few minutes and go watch this eight-minute video, then come back to the book,

http://bit.ly/1O6afgl

2. Understand difference between someone's position and their interests.

a. Position - what a person wants, it is concrete, tangible and can be visualized. Usually these are specific solutions a person wants and often they do not want to consider any other options.

b. Interests - Underlying need or concern person is trying to have satisfied, person's concern, need, and/or desire, underneath a position.

3. Identify yours and each other's positions and interests. Yes, you need to take the time to understand your position and interests before you try to pinpoint the other IEP team members' position and interests.

4. It is usually easy to define a person's position because it is what they are suggesting for a solution, or what they think needs to be done next. It can be more challenging to dig deeper and discover why they are proposing that solution - what their interests are. Here are some open-ended questions you can ask to discover what is really important to yourself and others:

- What changes would you like to see happen?

- How is this affecting the child?

- What is the felt experience below the surface the person is longing for?

- What about the current situation concerns you the most?

- Can you help me understand what the solution would accomplish?

- In what ways is that important to you?

5. Another way to identify yours and the other person's interests is to use this strategy developed by Nicholas Martin, Director of The Center for Accord and author of *A Guide to Collaboration For IEP Teams*. He recommends using two simple words, *So that*. When a teacher says, "I don't want parents always volunteering in the classroom where their child is." If you say, "so that..." this gives the teacher a chance to add to her comments. The teacher might reply, "So students can develop some independence from their parents." Aha, now you know the teacher's interest, student independence. Note: it may take saying *So that* several times in order to get to the most underlying concern.

6. Once interests are identified, the team can have a discussion about the interest(s). Continue the dialogue until everyone has a clear understanding of the interest.

7. Look for common interests. Talking through everyone's interests helps the team discover ways that both parties' interests may overlap, complement, or are non-competitive.

8. Prioritize the team's interests.

9. Generate possible solutions that are advantageous to both sides. Here are some important ground rules to follow when brainstorming:

• Begin with open-ended questions, such as: "How can we best.....?" or "What is the most agreeable way for us to ...?"

• Both parties need to suspend evaluating possible options and making judgments. If not, creative solutions will not be discovered.

• Be open to multiple options. If not, it is unlikely you will find a solution that will address the interests of both parties.

• Eliminate "the pie is only so big" thinking. If not, you will not reach the ability to see that both interests can be met.

• Agree that having both parties' interests (underlying needs) met is critical. Recognize it will take a collaborative effort to do so.

10. Collaboratively, determine the criteria to evaluate options.

11. Choose an option to try, implement it, and evaluate how it is working.

SCENARIO:

Parent:

I want my child to have a full-time aide that works with her.

Special Education Teacher:

I'm sorry, we don't have the budget to hire more staff.

Parent:

I know you can't use budget as an excuse. My child had a full time aide at her other school and I want her to have that here.

Special Education Teacher:

Research shows having a full time aide for a child can be detrimental to them learning independence. How do you see an aide helping your daughter?

Parent:

Well, one thing, the aide can help my daughter not be bullied on the playground. My daughter can run off the playground if other kids tease her. And my daughter needs extra help during reading in the classroom. An aide could help with all of those things.

Special Education Teacher:

An aide may be helpful keeping your daughter safe and supporting her learning. What I have found helpful in the past is to brainstorm some other ways we can make sure your child is safe on the playground and is more successful in reading.

Parent:

Well, I know there are a lot of kids on the playground at recess and not many adults to watch them. And I know the classroom teacher has a lot of other kids in the class to teach.

Special Education Teacher:

Let's take the playground situation first. One way to keep your daughter safe might be to hire a full time aide for her. Or, how about if we had an extra aide assigned recess duty when your child is outside to make sure she doesn't get bullied or runs away?

Parent:

I suppose we could try that. But what about help for reading? She needs an aide to help her understand her reading work.

Special Education Teacher:

I think it would be helpful if we had a conversation with her classroom teacher and see what her strengths are in reading and when the instruction from the teacher would be enough. We can also talk about where she struggles and how she might receive some pre-teaching or re-teaching of some of the skills, or help doing her seat-work from a peer buddy, have the special education teacher co-teaching with the classroom teacher during the reading block, or some other ideas we may come up with.

Parent:

I just don't want this to go on forever and it takes a long time before we actually sit down and talk with the classroom teacher.

Special Education Teacher:

I understand. I will talk with the teacher and see when she would be available in the next few days. What time of day works best for you to meet?

Parent:

Before or after school works good since I drive Selena to school each day.

Special Education Teacher:

Great, I'll give you a call with the day and time we can meet. I will also talk to the principal about setting up a meeting to amend her IEP so we make sure she is safe on the playground and is more successful in reading.

ANALYSIS:

The parent began the conversation by stating her position, "I want my child to have a full time aide that works with her." The teacher was able to help identify what the parent's interests were: her daughter being safe on the playground and be successful in reading.

Instead of only wanting to consider the solution the parent walked in the door with, she was willing to consider other options. Being open to new possibilities can lead to an even greater solution.

Sometimes we forget conflict is natural and occurs in many situations in our lives. Out of conflict can come positive change. The trick is how you manage conflict. Your reaction can either escalate or decrease the intensity of the conflict. Gerry Spence in *How To Argue And Win Every Time* makes these suggestions:

1. Begin to think as a storyteller. Visualize the story yourself. You do not have to memorize anything because you know the whole story.

2. Build your story around a point of view. Ask yourself:

• What is the vision for my child? What does he need in order to have that life you visualize for him?

• What facts, what reasons, exists to support what my child needs?

• What is the story that brings all of the above together?

3. Revisit the vision you have for your child, or what his own vision is. Re-read your vision statement. Now, think in terms of specifics, what does he need this year so he can be one step closer to his vision?

4. Do more preparation for telling your story at an IEP meeting by gathering facts, documents, reasons why your child is entitled to what you think he needs.

5. Now, trim down the facts, documents and reasons you are going to actually use in your story. Make an outline of your story and for each main point, write the supporting evidence you have in case you need to share that with the other party.

6. Write out your story of why you child needs what you are asking for. By taking the time to write your story, you are reaffirming to yourself the importance of your child. You do not want to read it at the IEP meeting, but the act of writing can also help clarify what you want to verbally express.

7. Go over your written story many times. Rearrange it, edit it; make sure you have used descriptive phrases. You want the other party to not only hear your story, but to also connect on a visual and emotional level with your words.

8. Select a phrase, a slogan that can represent the heart of your story. The slogan can create a mental image more moving than all the words you speak.

Here are two more problem-solving tools, Solution Circles and Six Thinking Hats. These can be helpful to use before an IEP meeting so there is time to really drill down and define the issues, possible causes and possible solutions.

Any decisions reached in the problem solving sessions will need to be brought to the IEP meeting, agreed to, and written in the IEP. Because you know the 'ole saying, "Anything not written down did not happen and no one will be accountable for it".

Solution Circles

Got twenty-five minutes? Solution Circles can be a terrific tool to use. This was developed by Marsha Forest, Jack Pearpoint, and John O'Brien to help teams get unstuck. It works best with a group of six to ten people. Roles: Problem Presenter, Facilitator/Time Keeper, Note Taker, and everyone else are the Brainstormers.

Step 1 (5 minutes):

The Problem Presenter has five uninterrupted minutes to describe the problem. The Facilitator keeps time and makes sure no one interrupts. The Note Taker takes notes where everyone can see them. Everyone listens. If the Problem Presenter stops talking before the five minutes are up, everyone stays silent until the full five minutes passes. Why is this important? The Problem Presenter gets five uninterrupted minutes.

Step 2 (5 minutes):

The Brainstormers ask clarifying and probing questions (see Chapter 2 in this book). Questions are asked to understand the problem and underlying interests (see earlier information in this chapter about differences between positions and interests). Do not ask, have you tried questions.

Step 3 (5 minutes):

The Problem Presenter continues to listen without responding. Everyone else chimes in with ideas for creative solutions. This is not the time to clarify, give speeches, lectures, or advice. The facilitator must make sure this is purely a brainstorming time.

Step 4 (5 minutes):

Now the Problem Presenter leads the entire group in a conversation. This is the time to further explore and/or clarify the possible solutions. It is important to focus on the positive points only instead of what cannot be done.

Step 5 (5 minutes):

The Problem Presenter and the group decide on the next steps that can be accomplished within the next three days. This can be the deal breaker. Research shows that unless a first step is taken almost immediately, people do not change their way of always doing things. Someone from the group volunteers to phone or talk to the Problem Presenter within three days and check if the first step has been taken.

You may be doubtful that a problem can be solved in twenty-five minutes, but try it. This is a very focused method, and many teams have been excited about the results.

Here is a handout you can share with others interested in trying Solution Circles. Go to   http://bit.ly/1MEqQUc   to download it.

Edward de Bono's Six Thinking Hats

You and your team members can learn how to examine an issue in multiple ways. I know, you are probably thinking, our team cannot even look at issues in one way. Everyone has felt frustrated by inefficient, wasteful meetings that are plagued by divisive arguments, lack of preparation, side conversations, and inaction but keep reading, this strategy works.

Edward de Bono is an international expert in the field of creative thinking. He developed the Six Thinking Hats technique. Instead of arguing between two existing possibilities, the Six Thinking Hats technique encourages participants to create new possibilities to consider. Instead of us vs. them de Bono's strategy has everyone work together to explore all sides of an issue.

Each way of thinking is identified with a colored symbolic "thinking hat." By mentally wearing and switching "hats," the group can easily focus, be redirected if needed, and look at an issue from different viewpoints.

In meetings, the Six Thinking Hats strategy has the benefit of blocking the confrontations that happen when people with different thinking styles discuss the same problem. This problem solving method provides a structure to help people think clearly by directing their thinking in one direction at a time.

In a group setting, each member thinks using the same thinking hat, at the same time, on the same problem. This is focused parallel thinking - a tool that facilitates creativity and collaboration. It enables each person's unique point of view to be included and considered. Argument and endless discussions can become a thing of the past. Thinking becomes more thorough.

Edward de Bono, teaches parallel thinking as an alternative to argument. Parallel thinking guides the thought processes in one direction at a time so you can effectively analyze issues, generate new ideas, and make better decisions. Read on to learn more about the Six Thinking Hats strategy.

1. Blue Hat: Overview: Where are we now? What have we done so far? What are we trying to do?

The Blue Hat is used to manage the thinking process. It is the control mechanism that ensures the Six Thinking Hats guidelines are observed. The Blue Hat stands for process control. This is the hat worn by people chairing meetings. When running into difficulties because ideas are running dry, they may direct activity into Green Hat thinking. When contingency plans are needed, they will ask for Black Hat thinking, etc.

Blue Hat Thinking: Process is the focus

• Thinking about thinking

• What thinking is needed?

• Organizing the thinking

• Planning for action

2. White Hat: Information: What are the facts? What information do we need to get? What is most important? How valid is this?

The White Hat calls for information known or needed. "The facts, just the facts." With this thinking hat, you focus on the data available. Look at the information you have, and see what you can learn from it. Look for gaps in your knowledge, and either try to fill them or take account of them. This is where you analyze past trends.

White Hat Thinking: Facts are the focus

• Information and data

• Neutral and objective

• What do I know?

• What do I need to find out?

• How will I get the information I need?

3. Green Hat: New ideas/creativity: What new ideas are possible? What can we create? What are some possible ways to work this out?

The Green Hat focuses on creativity; the possibilities, alternatives, and new ideas. It is an opportunity to express new concepts and new perceptions. This is where you can develop creative solutions to a problem. It is a freewheeling way of thinking, in which there is little criticism of ideas. A whole range of creativity tools can help you here.

Green Hat Thinking: Creativity is the focus.

• Ideas, alternatives, possibilities

• Options, solutions

4. Yellow Hat: Benefits/Assessing Value: What are the good points? What are the benefits?

The Yellow Hat symbolizes brightness and optimism. Under this hat you explore the positives and probe for value and benefit. The yellow hat helps you to think positively. It is the optimistic viewpoint that helps you see all the benefits of the decision and the value in it. Yellow Hat thinking helps you to keep going when everything looks gloomy and difficult.

Yellow Hat Thinking: Benefits are the focus.

• Positives, plus points

• Logical reasons are given

5. Black Hat: Judgment/Weak points: Will it work? Who does it affect? What is the evidence to support this?

The Black Hat is judgment - the devil's advocate or why something may not work. Spot the difficulties and dangers; where things might go wrong. Probably the most powerful and useful of the Hats, but it can be a problem if overused. Using black hat thinking, look at all the bad points of the decision. Look at it cautiously and defensively. Try to see why it might not work. This is important because it highlights the weak points in a plan.

It allows you to eliminate them, alter them, or prepare contingency plans to counter them.

Black Hat thinking helps to make your plans 'tougher' and more resilient. It can also help you spot fatal flaws and risks before you embark on a course of action. Black Hat thinking is one of the real benefits of this technique, as many successful people get so used to thinking positively they often cannot see problems in advance. This leaves them under-prepared for difficulties.

Black Hat Thinking: Cautions are the focus.

- Difficulties, weaknesses, dangers

- Logical reasons are given.

- Spotting the risks

6. Red Hat: Gut feelings: How do I feel about this right now?

The Red Hat signifies feelings, hunches and intuition. When using this hat you can express emotions and feelings and share fears, likes, dislikes, loves, and hates. 'Wearing' the red hat, you look at problems using intuition, gut reaction, and emotion. Also try to think how other people will react emotionally. Try to understand the responses of people who do not fully know your reasoning.

Red Hat Thinking: Feelings are the focus.

- Intuition, hunches, gut instinct

- People's feelings right now.

- Reasons are not given.

Blue Hat: Summarize: What will we do next? What decisions have we reached? Go back to the person wearing the blue hat and have them summarize the process.

Benefits of Using Six Thinking Hats:

• Look at problems, decisions, and opportunities systematically

• Generate more, better ideas and solutions

• Make meetings much shorter and more productive

• Reduce conflict among team members or meeting participants

• Create dynamic, results oriented meetings that make people want to participate

• Go beyond the obvious to discover effective alternate solutions

• Spot opportunities where others see only problems

• Think clearly and objectively

• View problems from new and unusual angles

• Make thorough evaluations

• See all sides of a situation

• Achieve significant and meaningful results

CALL TO ACTION:

Tired of the frustration and feeling like you never get anywhere in IEP meetings? Do you want to learn more about how to use the ideas and strategies in this book at your next IEP meeting?

I am designing a series of online classes to help guide parents like you to be more effective advocates for their child. Interested? Email me at charmaine@cspeda.com and learn more about the classes. You'll be such a better advocate for your child! Your child will be the winner!

RESOURCES:

A Guide to Collaboration For IEP Teams by Nicholas Martin

Crucial Conversations: Tools for Talking When Stakes Are High by Kerry Patterson, Joseph Grenny, Ron McMillan, and Al Swizzler

Getting to Yes, by Roger Fisher and William Ury

How to Argue And Win Every Time by Gerry Spence

Want to add some terrific creative thinking tools to your toolbox? You'll learn specific techniques that can be so useful in all aspects of your life! Visit http://bit.ly/1YiJJ6p to learn more.

BONUS:

Go to http://0s4.com/r/DW6PZR to download a poster that will help you remember to create more possibilities for your child.

If you want to go FAST, go alone.

If you want to go far, go TOGETHER.

        African Proverb

Chapter 7: The End is Really the Beginning

When you reach the end of what you should know,

you will be at the beginning of what you should sense.

Kahlil Gibran

What you want at the end of your child's school career, what your child wants his future to be, is the end you must begin today.

Stay focused on the Big Picture. This is about your child. Make sure you judge decisions by this one criteria: Is this decision aligned to our long-term vision for our child? That end vision you have, the one your child has, is what should be driving each plan written for your child. Each plan should be one step closer to your vision, not away from it.

So, get clear on your vision and be able to communicate it effectively. You want to be able to describe your vision in detail to build a complete and powerful mental image of that rich and fulfilling life you child deserves.

As this book comes to a close, it is time to take action on all the things you have learned. If you highlighted certain sentences or if you jotted down notes in the margin as you were reading this book, go back and re-read those parts. Decide how you can incorporate these steps in your next meeting with the school staff.

At the end of each chapter there is a Call to Action. Have you done those? If not, stop, go back to each chapter and complete each Call to Action.

Are there particular topics you would like to explore more? Look up some of the resources listed at the end of each chapter. Now that you know more, you need to act on that new knowledge in order to continue making positive differences for your child.

WHY:

We need to continue to see the end goal and know our everyday actions are making a difference for our children.

WHAT PARENTS CAN DO:

1. After each school meeting, think about what you learned, and what you want to make sure you do again at the next meeting. Also, make note of what you want to avoid doing again at meetings.

2. Think outside of the IEP boxes. The IEP meeting is not an exercise in filling out forms or making sure there is something written in every box on the IEP. Put your child first. For every decision made, ask yourself, is this decision based on what my child needs now and for her future?

3. Write down the outcomes for your child that you want to celebrate at the end of each school year. Do periodic check-ins with the staff throughout the year to see if everyone is on the same page and if your child is one step closer to reaching his goals.

4. Let the dreams you have for your child guide your thoughts, beliefs, and actions!

5. Practice painting a picture with your words, of your WHY your child deserves what you are asking for. In order to win people's hearts and minds, you must begin with their hearts - the WHY.

6. Remember what your child hears about herself; what you share about her with staff members, and what you believe is possible for your child, makes all the difference in the world.

7. Share your high expectations of your child, academically and socially, with your child, other family members and his teachers.

8. Hold tight to your dreams. Believe in possibilities. Show your child their dreams count.

As a parent of an adult son who happens to have Down syndrome, I hope you are adjusting your dreams for your child. I hope you now realize there are so many more opportunities for children with disability labels than there were just a few years ago.

I hope you now understand you can look at the same information everyone else is looking at and yet see something different.

You need to act, feel, and perform according to what you believe is true for your child. What you believe is true becomes true.

CALL TO ACTION:

Be good to yourself! Give yourself credit for all that you do!

RESOURCES:

The Book of Doing and Being: Rediscovering Creativity in Life, Love, and Work by Barnet Bain

BONUS:

Call me at 208-340-5874 for a free thirty-minute phone conversation.

Chances are, I have experienced the emotions, or similar ones, that you are feeling and we'll relate to each other. I am here to help parents advocate for their child. When there is a gap between what the school is proposing and what you feel is needed, let me help you bridge that gap.

> *What you want at the end of your child's school career,*
>
> *what your child wants his future to be,*
>
> *is the end you must begin today.*
>
> — Charmaine Thaner

- **Note:** My goal in writing this book is to reach many more parents than I can with my individual advocacy work I do. If you found some tips and strategies that will help you speak up for your child, please post a review on the Amazon page for my book. http://amzn.to/1NFAC8p

About The Author

Everything Charmaine does is because she believes life can be better. She works with and learns from parents of school-age children with disabilities by providing tools and strategies so their children receive the education they deserve.

Charmaine's diverse experiences provide a unique perspective when collaborating with families and educators. She is the parent of a young adult who received special education services. She has supported students, parents and educators as a special educator, classroom teacher, parent advocate, and adjunct university instructor. She continues to support parents as an advocate and public speaker.

Contact Charmaine at

charmaine@cspeda.com

www.cspeda.com

Made in the USA
Columbia, SC
12 January 2018